OLDIES BUT GOODIES

**1910
GARDEN
PARTY
DRESS**
(See
page 195.)

OLDIES BUT GOODIES

How to restyle yesterday's clothing and castoffs into exciting new fashions for today.

by Donna Lawson

with interior photography by Dick Swift

Butterick Publishing

Illustrations by Rick and Glory Brightfield
Book Design by Sheila Lynch
Cover Design by Sallie Baldwin

Library of Congress Catalog Card Number: 76-57296
International Standard Book Number: 0-88421-032-4
Copyright © 1977 by Butterick Publishing
161 Sixth Avenue, New York, New York 10013
A Division of American Can Company

PRINTED IN U.S.A.

To my Pa, who always is a regular clotheshorse.

And to the clotheshorses (God love them) Harriet Dacey and Jane MacLeod Pappidas, who gave extra special help, Mary Orser, who turned over her house, Nona Luna, Zubin and baby Zandra, Barbara Greenberg, Olga Rosenberger, Aimee and Fran Swift, Savitri Brightfield and her mom and dad, Cheyenne Swain-Borov, Corinne van Plaar, Teresa Savilla, Cheina, Dejha, Bobbie Pearlman and baby Lexie, Bobbie Abrams, Alex Aames, Joni Minter, Parvati, Barcat, to all those lovers of rags like Helen L. Swain and Shahastra who lured me into their fantasy, to the Salvation Army and Goodwill Industries, in particular to Dick Swift for his patience, to Rick and Glory for theirs, to Peter Hughes, who knows how to spell *snugly,* to me, who worked hard, and to you, for whom I hope making-do will become a creative passion.

MAMA'S
PETTICOAT

(See
page 109.)

CONTENTS

7

WHAT'S THIS BOOK ABOUT?

I'll tell you. This book is about making silk purses out of sows' ears—or recycling old clothes and accessories and doing it with class.

And it's about places to get materials: flea markets, church sales, thrift shops, antique and free stores, the Salvation Army, and Goodwill Industries.

And it's about attics and basements and trading clothes with friends.

And it's about saving money, looking unique, and having fun putting the whole thing together.

Just last Saturday, I had a fine time wheeling and dealing at a flea market. I bought a 1930's crepe blouse for $2.50, a satin stocking case to make an evening bag (see page 134) for $1.50, and a pair of beaded mocassins for fifty cents.

And that's me (in the photo at left) shopping at the Salvation Army. The pile of clothes that I'm hugging was a veritable gold mine. The bronze sequined dress (to turn into a jacket) by itself made my day.

Sometimes you can wear your old finds as is. And other times they cry for your own invention. I run my creations through a zigzag sewing machine with the bravado of a trapeze artist.

You never approach old clothes timidly. After all, they're cheap. If you make the wrong cut, you haven't lost a fortune. And you can always turn your mistakes into something grand, like a patchwork thing or other.

There's always some wonderful rag in my bottom drawer—a hand-embroidered dresser scarf, a pair of 1940's chintz

11

drapes, an old house dress in a great print—to whip into something fantastic.

I'm always well stocked because I love the hunt. It becomes addictive. Once you get into it, you'll find yourself poking around in dusty old thrift shop bins whenever you get the chance.

Now, wearing old clothes doesn't have to become a lifestyle. You don't throw out your whole wardrobe or stop buying anything new or making clothes from scratch.

But it's dramatic and stylish to add a piece here and there. Kids love new things made up from old, especially when it's a great sun dress made from Daddy's shirt (page 89). These new concoctions from timeworn materials make wonderful gifts, too.

People who love wearing old clothes are romantics. They're nostalgic for the past. They like the history that many of these old clothes carry with them. And they find adventure now and then in pulling together something out of nothing. They are, I think, people like me, who find aesthetic appeal in occasionally making a beautiful meal from leftovers.

If you're one of these people (and I'll bargain you are, if you've read this far), then welcome to this book. There are fascinating projects and a lot of fun among its pages.

1
MAKEOVERS

Would you ever think that a 1960's mini, your aged kimono, a bunch of has-been ties or scarves, your husband's old shirts, or Grandpa's union suit could have new life?

They can. Coming up, you'll learn to turn bottom-drawer and back-closet discards into snappy "new" clothes. The clothes are shown before and after, just like magazine beauty pages. "This is how it was," say the pages. "This is what you can end up with."

Some of the results are frankly stunning. Some are plain functional. Others are whimsical. Each will save you money. And while you're at it, you'll have fun. And the projects will turn you on to your own ideas.

Pantskirts Forever

First we thought of making skirts from blue jeans. And that idea took off like wild flowers. Now it's extended to making skirts from every possible kind of pants.

You can make a gorgeous winter skirt from woolen Navy pants, and a summer one from tropical resort pants. But it doesn't have to stop here. Once you've caught on, you'll see that wool tweeds, gabardines, or comfortably broken-in corduroys have potential as skirts.

So take another look at those too-short, too-big, too-small, tapered, or just plain out-of-style pants. Realize that you're starting with a waistband, often pockets, and enough length for a skirt. Take it from there. You may have to use two pairs of pants to get the proper width or mid-calf length. Start swiping them from your dad or boyfriend. Or pick up a few spare pairs at your local thrift shop, freestore, flea market, or garage sale.

13

before

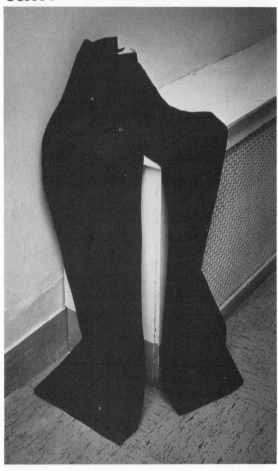

SAILOR PANTSKIRT

Two pairs of Navy pants are needed to make a long pantskirt like the one in the picture. A short skirt takes only one pair. The pants that we used cost approximately ten dollars each secondhand at an Army-Navy store. The machine-embroidery pieces were found at a thrift shop, and cost ten cents each. They gave a Slavic look to the finished skirt. Embroidery can also be cut from another "found" garment or stitched directly onto the skirt. (See page 62 for more old embroidery uses.)

1. To make the long sailor pantskirt, stitching was removed from the hem and inseam of one pair of pants 35″ long. (Corinne, who wears these, is *six feet* tall; measure yours according to your height.) Then the center front seam was opened up to a point 10″ down from the top of the buttoned panel. This skirt measured 33″ from

1.

front, inside out

take
out
inseams

trim away
excess

pin down center

the top of the waistband. (A 28″ length would make it a short skirt, which would require only one pair of pants.)

2. From the second pair of pants, a rectangle measuring $6\frac{1}{2}''$ by $24\frac{1}{2}''$ was cut. This was the insert for the front pleat. (If the skirt was to be short, this piece would measure $6\frac{1}{2}''$ by $19\frac{1}{2}''$, and the leg from the one pair of pants could be used.) The skirt was laid flat, inside out. The leg inseams were pinned together in a straight line down the center front, using the entire width of the pants legs at the skirt hem. A $\frac{5}{8}''$ overlap was left for the seam allowance. Excess fabric was trimmed away. The long sides of the rectangle were tucked under $\frac{5}{8}''$ for the seam allowance and pinned. Then the skirt was machine stitched two rows through the three thicknesses of cloth, leaving $1\frac{1}{2}''$ of hem unstitched.

2.

rectangle
$6\frac{1}{2}''$ x $24\frac{1}{2}''$

stitch through
3 layers

3.

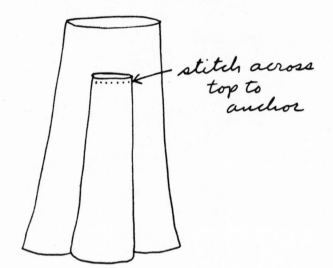

stitch across
top to
anchor

4. back, rightside out

27"

trim off and
sew seam straight
up back

5.

front, rightside out

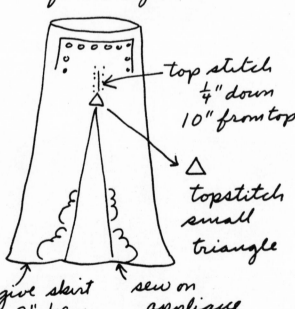

top stitch
¼" down
10" from top

topstitch
small
triangle

give skirt
2" hem

sew on
appliqué

3. The top of the front pleat was machine stitched to anchor it, and the pleat was pinned closed. Then the skirt was turned right side out.

4. The skirt back was then pinned and the excess fabric trimmed from the back, so that the skirt measured 27" straight across the hem when finished.

5. A 2" hem was made. The skirt was topstitched $\frac{1}{4}$" out on either side of the center seam, 10" down from top buttons. A small triangle was topstitched right at the point where the pleat began. The machine-embroidery pieces were cut into curved shapes, then arranged around the outside of the pleat. Feather stitching attached them to the skirt.

SAILOR
PANTSKIRT
after

before

TROPICAL PANTSKIRT

The pants by Lily Pulitzer (a Palm Beach designer) at one time fit a gentleman who hobnobbed in Key West. They were found there in a thrift shop and bought for seventy-five cents.

1. To make the skirt, the pants legs were cut off at the desired skirt length.
2. Then the legs were slit up to the crotch inseam on both sides.
3. The crotch area was trimmed away so that there were open triangles on both sides of the skirt (up to the zipper in front).

18

1.

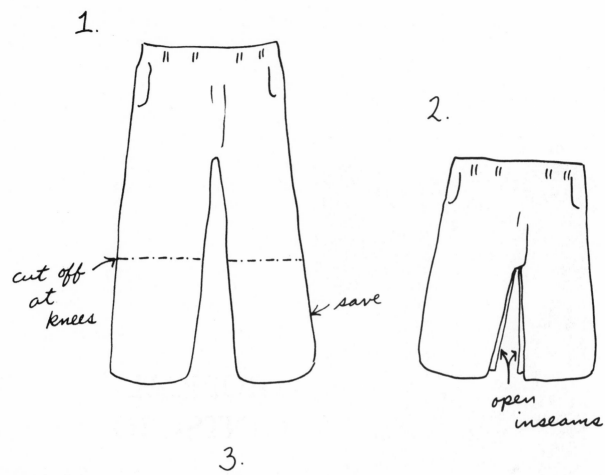

cut off at knees

save

2.

open inseams

3.

trim away excess

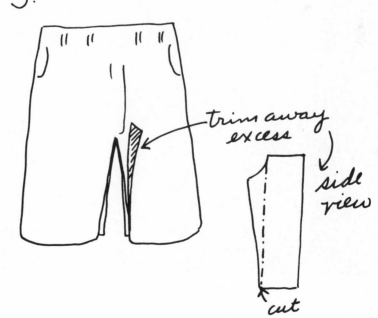

side view

cut

4.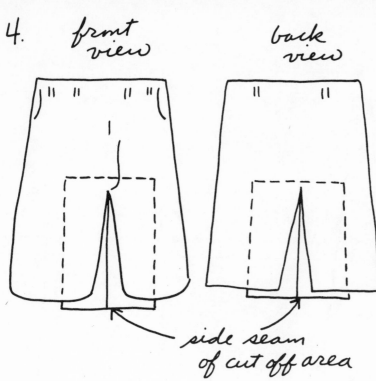

front view   back view

side seam
of cut off area

5.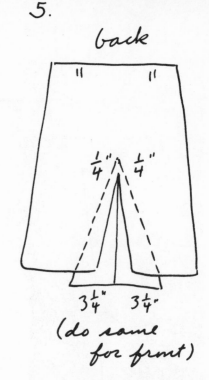

back

$\frac{1}{4}''$ $\frac{1}{4}''$

$3\frac{1}{4}''$ $3\frac{1}{4}''$

(do same
for front)

6.

inside back

$\frac{1}{4}''$ seam

(do same
for front)

4. The pants were laid flat on the floor. The "cut-off" parts of the legs were opened up on one side and, with the remaining seam in the middle, were placed so that one cut-off piece was under each of the open triangles.

5. To get the kick pleat effect, each triangle opening was made $6\frac{1}{2}''$ wider at the bottom, and $1''$ wider at the top.

6. Then the cut-off pieces were sewn into the open triangle areas of the pants, allowing a $\frac{1}{4}''$-seam all the way around. Next the pleat was pressed flat. It now measured $3''$ wide at the bottom, tapering to $\frac{1}{4}''$ at the top.

7. Then the pantskirt was topstitched $\frac{1}{4}''$ in from the edge around each triangle and $\frac{1}{4}''$ in from the hemline, and each triangle was stitched through the three thicknesses down about $2''$ from the top point.

75¢ TROPICAL PANTSKIRT

after

21

before

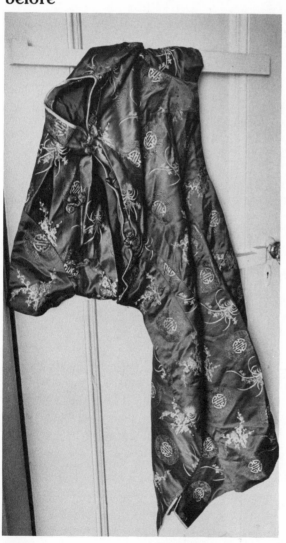

MARY'S CHINESE MINI

Mary Orser is a professional astrologer whose clothing tastes run to the romantic, oriental, and exotic. The Chinese mini was found on sale at the local secondhand clothing store for fifty cents. It was too short and had too many tucks at the waist and unattractive cap sleeves. But the fabric was beautiful heavily embossed red silk (the high-energy color Mary wanted). She turned it over to her neighbor Shahastra's nimble fingers and it turned into the gorgeous oriental jacket. (For a nifty way to recycle a miniskirt into a child's jumper, turn to page 93.)

1. There were four darts in the front of the dress and four in back.
2. Shahastra took them out. Then she pressed out the creases. Next, she cut the bottom part of the dress off right below the hip. She removed the cap sleeves.

1.

original darts

2.

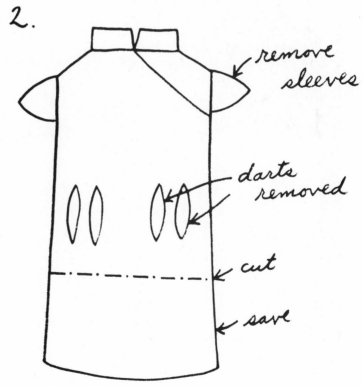

remove sleeves

darts removed

cut

save

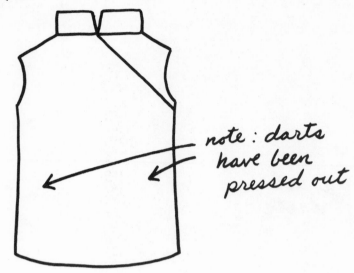

2a.

note : darts have been pressed out

3.

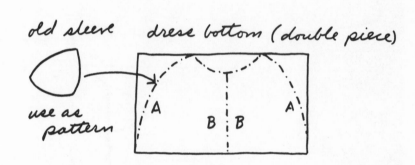

old sleeve   *dress bottom (double piece)*

use as pattern

A   A

B B

3. The bottom piece of the dress, including the side slits, was used to make new sleeves. The cap sleeves were used as a pattern for outside (A) and inside (B) curves. One of the original cap sleeves was stitched into a purse and a zipper and tassel added to it.

24

MARY'S
CHINESE
MINI

after

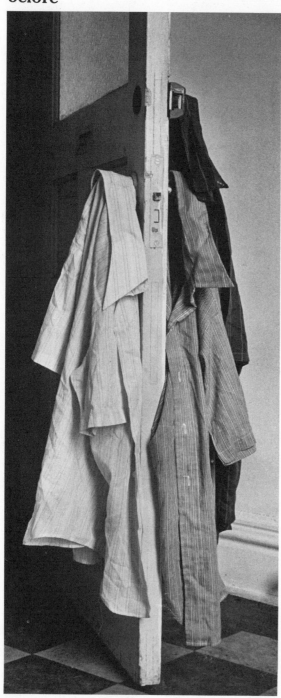

THREE-SHIRT SHORTS OUTFIT

The purple, rust, and blue stripes of the three-shirt combination looked Middle Eastern. The fabric was soft and summery. The shirts, fifty cents each at Goodwill Industries, seemed to work naturally into a shorts outfit.

The shirt with the pale blue stripes fit just as it was, so it became the basic shirt. To create a mixture of stripes, the collar of the pale basic shirt was replaced by a rust-colored one. And the lower sleeve edges of the purple shirt were cut off and sewn onto the pale ones. Then, using a basic commercial pattern, or cutting

$1.50

after

around a pair of shorts that fit, the rust striped shirt was used for one side of the shorts, the purple for the other. The pockets were reversed, rust pocket on purple side of shorts and vice versa. A combination of the two striped fabrics made a drawstring tie which pulled through a casing at the top of the shorts. (A little girl's sun dress is made from her daddy's shirt on page 89.)

27

before

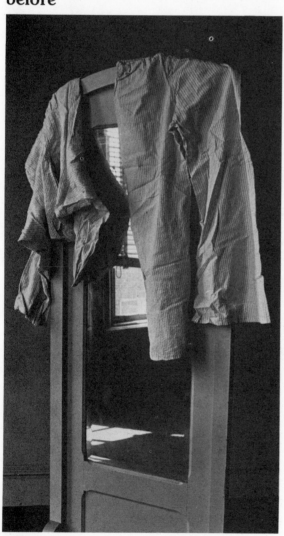

BETTER BAGGY

The seersucker pants outfit originated at a freestore. There was too much yellow and it was ordinary, so the pants were dyed green and made baggy. These days bagginess is all the rage. Here's how it was done. The pants were the right length, so Harriet opened up a stitch or two at the bottom of each side seam and ran elastic through the hemmed edge. Then she adjusted the pieces of elastic to fit the ankle and sewed them together. Now she had a whole other pair of pants.

FREE

after

before

A CHINESE COLLAR

1. Harriet took an ordinary notched lapel collar.
2. She put one lapel (the left) inside of the garment and, after establishing the position with a pin, attached a snap. Then she put the other lapel (the right) outside of the garment and attached it with another snap. Next she put two more snaps at the waistline to catch and hold the loose fabric so it didn't flop.

1.

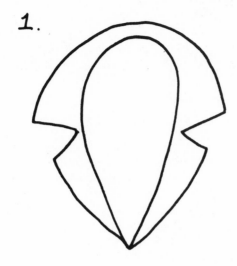

2.

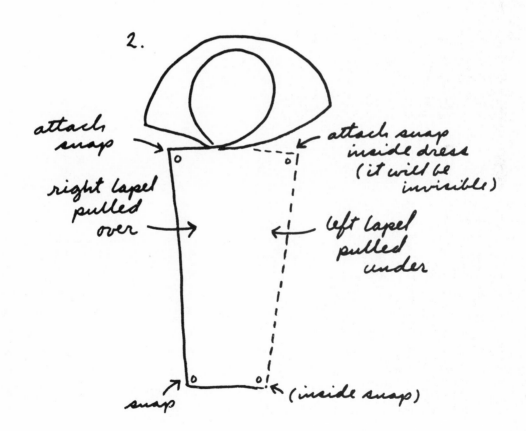

attach snap

attach snap
inside dress
(it will be
invisible)

right lapel
pulled
over

left lapel
pulled
under

snap

(inside snap)

3.

collar unfolded

fold under

4.

fold collar
points in

5.

attach small
hook at top
of collar
(if necessary)

3. Then she took the collar, unfolded it, and made it stand up behind the neck.
4. Then she folded the top of the collar under until it met the seam that attached it to the dress top.
5. The points of the collar were folded under so that they were hidden between the front and back of the collar fabric. After pinning everything in place, she seamed the Chinese collar all the way around and attached a small hook and eye at the top. (If the fabric is stiff enough, it will stand by itself.)

FREE CHINESE COLLAR
after

before

TWELVE TIES
Color Plate 2

Twelve wide cotton and silk ties were collected in thrift shops all over the country. Each cost about twenty-five cents, the set totaling about three dollars.

The linings were removed from each tie; then the ties were pressed out flat, with the wider parts at the bottom, the narrower ones at the top. Then they were basted together. (At this point, much of the development of this skirt depends on the individual figure. A bigger person will need more ties to go around her than a smaller one. A small one will need fewer than a medium-size person.) The tops of the ties were cut off at a point where they

34

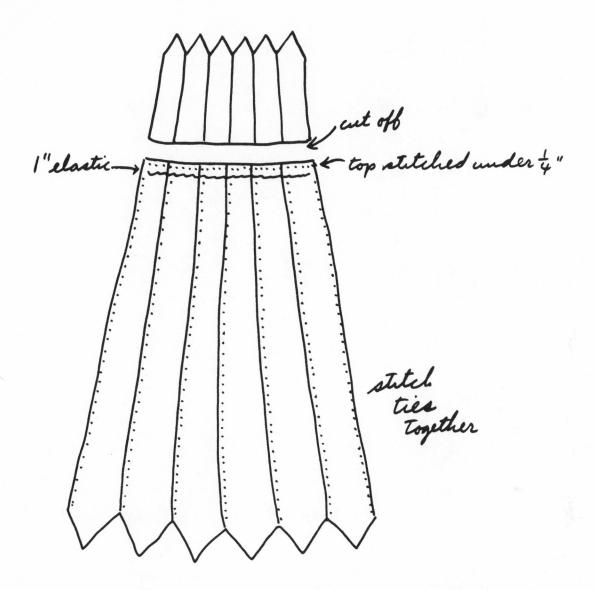

cut off

1" elastic →

← top stitched under $\frac{1}{4}$"

stitch
ties
together

formed a waistline. Then the ties were permanently stitched together. (The wide, pointed ends were already hemmed. A 6" placket was left at one side.) The top was stitched under $\frac{1}{4}$", and a 1"-wide elastic was stitched into the waistband so it fit snugly against the waist. A hook and eye fastener was sewn at the side.

35

**TWELVE
TIES**

after

$3

GRANDPA'S UNION SUIT

These soft and cuddly long johns have been wardrobe basics for men in decades past and even today. And if you find them in a used-clothing bin, hang on tight. They make wonderful shirts and jackets—warm, funky, fun to wear, good to look at. These two worn by Nona and Barbara were from a freestore. The great big one was cut off jacket length and dyed bright blue. Barbara's was cut short and dyed green.

FREE

EIGHT SCARVES

Color Plate 1

They are often *real* silk. Sometimes they cost no more than ten cents each at thrift stores, although twenty-five cents to one dollar (for really special ones) is more like it. Think of it: put together they can make a total silk dress for one dollar—at worst ten dollars. This scarf dress cost nothing to make.

Jane MacLeod Pappidas had eight brightly colored scarves in her bottom drawer. One day she dug them out and put them to use as a floaty dress for her friend Teresa, who here shows a little leg but it could be worn over pants or a long skirt. All the scarves were square. One pair, measuring 28″ each, was positioned to make diamond shapes front and back (A and B). These were the starting pieces on which this puzzle-of-a-dress was built. (At this point, Jane cautions, "Except for

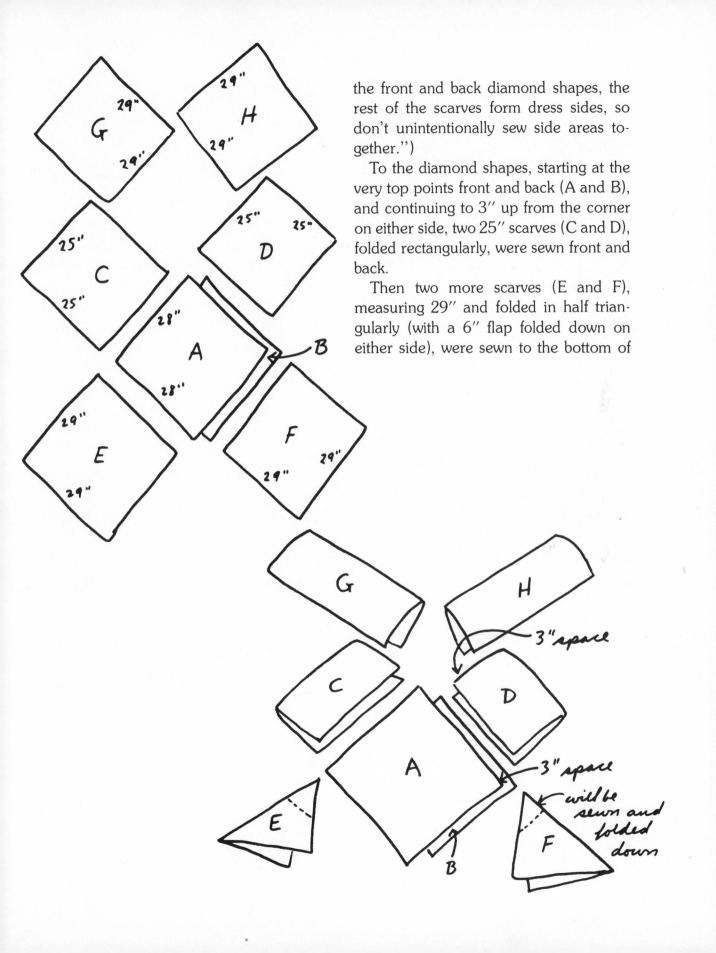

the front and back diamond shapes, the rest of the scarves form dress sides, so don't unintentionally sew side areas together.")

To the diamond shapes, starting at the very top points front and back (A and B), and continuing to 3″ up from the corner on either side, two 25″ scarves (C and D), folded rectangularly, were sewn front and back.

Then two more scarves (E and F), measuring 29″ and folded in half triangularly (with a 6″ flap folded down on either side), were sewn to the bottom of

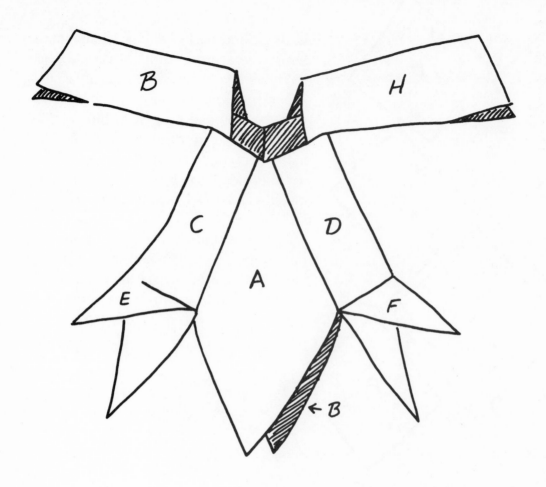

the folded rectangular shapes (C and D), then to the remaining 3″ on either sides of the diamond shapes (A and B).

The two remaining 29″ scarves (G and H) were stitched front and back to the top of the folded rectangular shape, leaving a 3″ space on each side of the top diamond point for the neckline (G).

Then at the points, scarves G and H were stitched together to within 9″ of each end. These last two scarves form the sleeves. A zigzag stitch bound the scarves together. But a hand or machine running stitch can be used.

FREE EIGHT
SCARVES
after

41

KIMONO FOR
FIVE CENTS

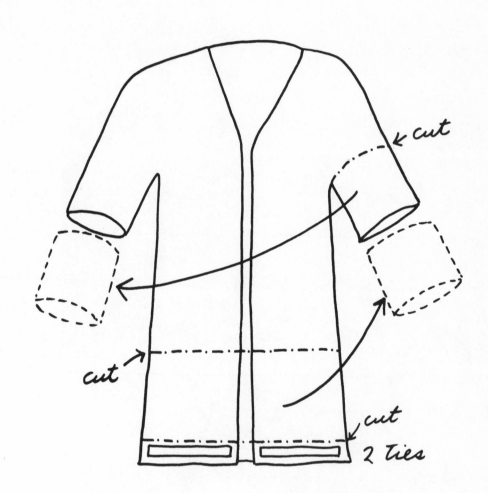

The kimono may have come from the Fifties. It was not old but had fetching red chrysanthemums on a black ground. So Bobbie bought it for five cents at a jumble sale (like a flea market) in England. What a price! As it was, it lacked style.

"Because kimono sleeves are short, and I wanted a long-sleeved blouse, I took out one sleeve and added it to the other. Then I cut off the bottom of the kimono and made the remaining sleeve. Last, I made two little ties to hold it together over pants." (See how a gorgeous old kimono became an evening coat on page 192.)

1.

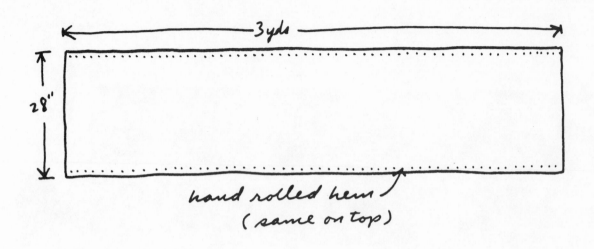

3 yds

28"

hand rolled hem
(same on top)

2.

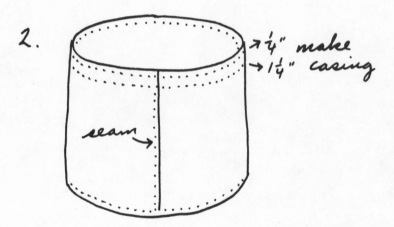

→ ¼" make
→ 1¼" casing

seam →

3.

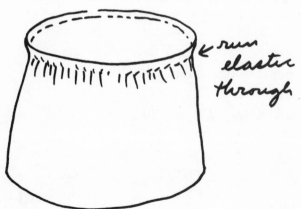

→ run elastic through

ONE BIG STOLE

This wide, three-yard-long, handmade white chiffon stole was bought for fifty cents at a flea market. It was hand rolled on both sides. So Bobbie seamed both ends together widthwise, stitched a casing ¼″ and again 1¼″ from the top edge, then ran a 1″-wide elastic through it. She wears it over a white leotard with an antique lace scarf.

before

A FLOUNCE MAKES GOOD

The pretty print mini with a flounce was bought at a thrift shop for one dollar.

1. The long back zipper was removed. The dress was cut off right under the armholes.
2. The darts were removed and the skirt pressed.

46

1.

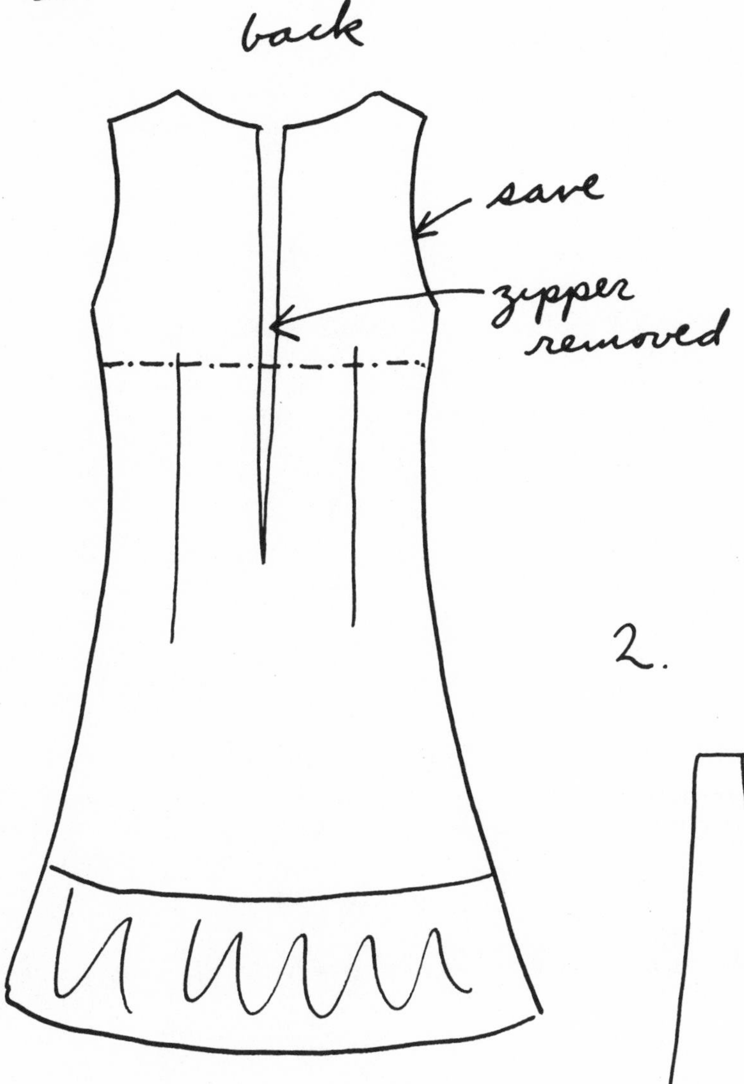

back

save

zipper
removed

2.

darts
removed

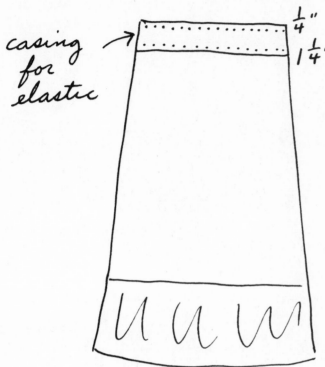

3.

casing
for
elastic

$\frac{1}{4}''$
$1\frac{1}{4}''$

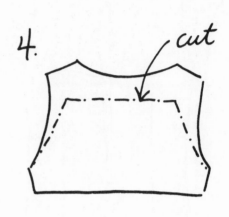

4.

cut

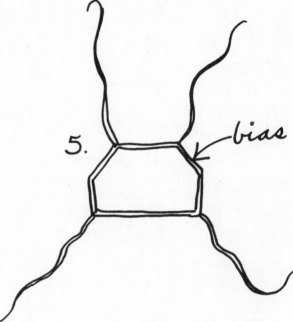

5.

bias

3. A casing was made at the skirt top by turning over a 2″ fold and stitching $\frac{1}{4}''$ and again $1\frac{1}{4}''$ from the top all around inside.

4. A drawstring was pulled through the casing and out through a small opening made in the center part of the skirt.

5. Then a halter top piece was cut out of the top.

6. Last, it was edged with yellow piping, to match the skirt edge. Piping also made straps, which were tied around the neck and across the back.

48

$1

A
FLOUNCE
MAKES
GOOD
after

49

before

BIG FLOP
TURNS SLEEK

Once ladies stayed home and wore pretty house dresses. Now ladies go to work and pretty house dresses are antiques. This one, bought in an antique clothing store for three dollars, was made in a nice cotton, better than most things you can find today. The oriental print, a black ground covered with tulips (yellow, orange, blue, green, and white), was in the mood of today's fashions. But the collar and cuffs were overpowering *and* in *bright* orange. Furthermore, the dress was two sizes too big.

1. So bravely (which is the only way to do it) Corinne slashed about 3″ from the back. Then she seamed it back together.
2. The sleeves were cut off the dress so more fabric could be taken from the shoulders and side seams.

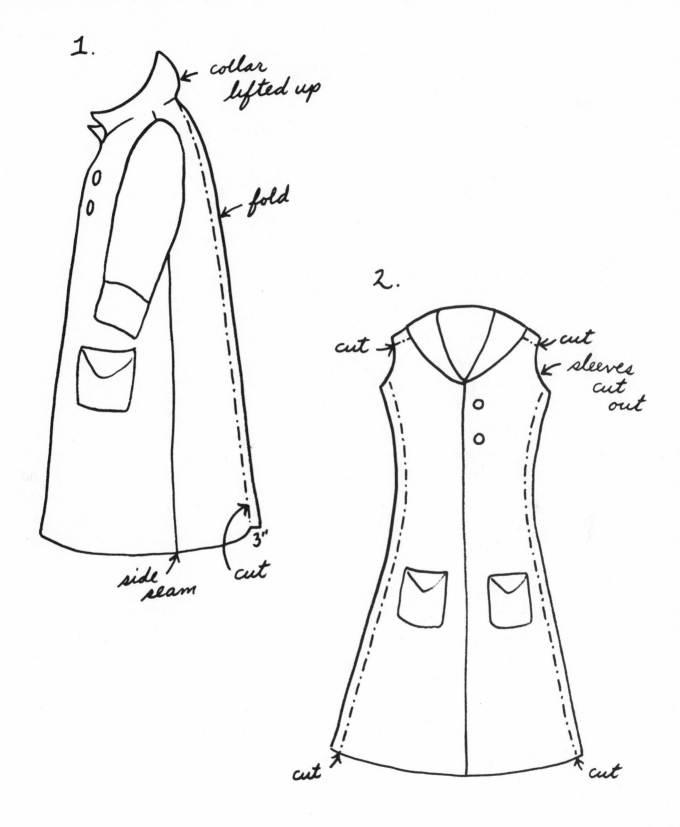

1.

collar
lifted up

fold

side
seam

cut

3"

2.

cut

cut
sleeves
cut
out

cut

cut

3.

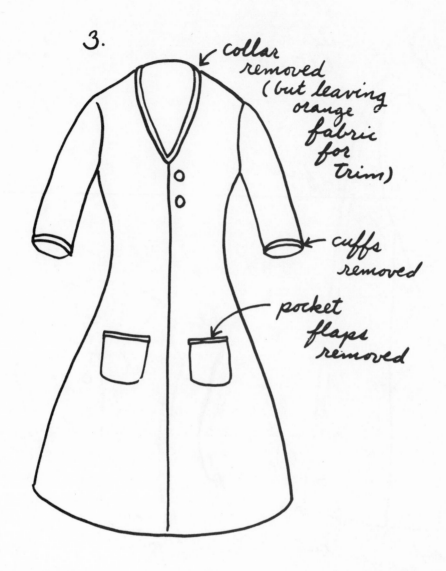

collar removed (but leaving orange fabric for trim)

cuffs removed

pocket flaps removed

3. The sleeves were sewn on again once the body of the dress was reduced. Then all that bright orange was cut down to a mere $\frac{3}{4}''$ edging which was turned under and zigzag stitched around the V-neckline, sleeves, and pocket edges. Now Corinne wears the house dress as a coat over ankle-tied jeans and a T-shirt.

$3

53

before

OLD NIGHTIE WITH NEW MEANING
Color Plate 4

Nightgowns go out on the town! They're worn as summer dresses, smocks over jeans, evening and wedding gowns. I've even seen flannel nighties shortened, dyed daytime colors like loden green or navy, and worn on the street when the weather turns cool.

Starchy and white, it began its life at the beginning of the twentieth century. But there it was—rumpled in the corner of an antique shop. Barbara saw its future as a summer dress. So she bought it for two dollars, mended a torn spot with iron-on-tape, dyed it a rosy hue, and embroidered around the neckline, using feather stitching and French knots. Barbara feels it's best to wash the gown in cold-water soap to preserve the precious old fibers.

"Old clothes are the only ones I like to wear," says Barbara. "They're broken in, comfortable, soft, and have character, like a finely aged person. New clothes haven't any personality. You look like everybody else when you wear them."

FRENCH KNOT

Bring thread up. Wind yarn around needle one to three times. Insert needle near the thread and hold thread firmly as you draw the needle down through the coiled thread.

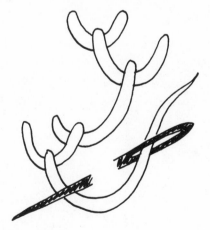

FEATHER STITCH

For first stitch, bring thread up. Make a diagonal stitch being sure to loop thread under the needle point. Pull through. Continue taking diagonal stitches first in one direction and then in the opposite direction.

Note: For other embroidery stitches to use, see instructions on pages 181, 186, and 187.

55

OLD
NIGHTIE
WITH
NEW
MEANING
 after

$2

Bathrobes Reborn

Take them off the bathroom door. Once they've worn out their shower-to-sheets use, make them into tunics, vests, or skirts. Or like one smart cookie I know, dye an old quilted robe, cut it off short, put frog fasteners on the front, and wear it as a Chinese-style jacket over pants.

ONCE A BATHROBE, NOW A TUNIC

The bathrobe was bought for $1.50. With sleeves, the robe lacked style. Without them it took on the character of a jazzy tunic. Armholes were cut down an extra 2″ on either side and hemmed. The belt was tied in back for added swagger. Worn over a shirt and ankle-tied jeans—mighty spiffy!

57

NOW A
TUNIC
after

$1.50

58

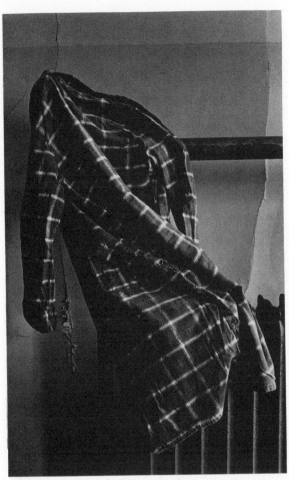

before

NOW A SKIRT

This one dollar bathrobe hung on the rack at the thrift store—red plaid flannel and toasty warm, but frumpy as all get out. But wait—the infinite possibilities—pockets, a placket, my yes, a skirt.

Before buying a bathrobe, fold the top part over under the armholes and hold it up to your waist to see if the pockets fall in the appropriate place and if there is enough length. Many robe styles and fabrics can be converted into skirts. If they button up the front, good enough—any detail can be utilized.

59

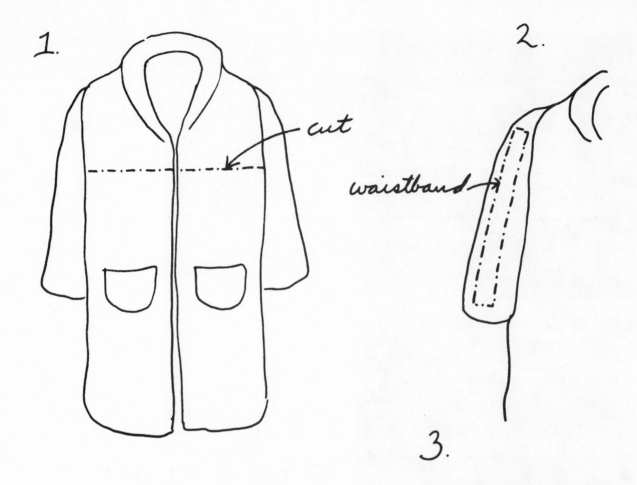

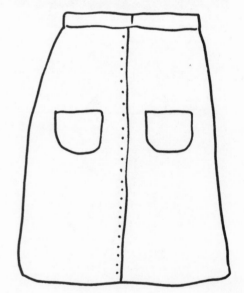

1. First, the robe was cut off straight under the armholes, then gathered to fit at the waistline.
2. A waistband was cut from a sleeve and attached to the skirt.
3. To make a 1″ placket, the front was stitched up to within 6″ of the top, and a snap or sewn-on fabric gripper put in.

$1.50   NOW
A SKIRT

after

Collecting Lace, Embroidery, and Other Handwork

Stitchery, crocheting, and embroidery were feminine occupations of yesterday. Ribbons and lace spoke of femininity—no woman was without them. She stored her stockings and lingerie in satin-stitched bags and kept sachets in her bureau drawers. This was before we were all in a rush.

Now all these fripperies are antiques, still to be found in thrift shops and flea markets at reasonable prices. But they're going fast—and the price will get higher as more recycling uses are found for them.

On the next pages: a pretty embroidered old hanky and two placemats turn into a camisole top; doilies make up into halter tops; lace coasters are sewn onto a T-shirt; old hand-crocheted pieces make a dress bodice; and antimacassars become jacket pockets. And you'll find still more projects in the "Everything That Isn't Pants, Skirts, Coats, and Dresses" chapter starting on page 127.

A HANKY CAMISOLE

On the next page Corinne wears a camisole top made from two linen placemats
(one yellow, one blue, each measuring
16″ × 11″) and a handkerchief (gold,
with lovely, colorful, French knot flowers
on it), which cost twenty-five cents.

The handkerchief was cut in half and
strips were cut from the middle for straps.
The remaining parts of each half (with
embroidery on them) were stitched across
the width of each placemat. Then the mats
were stitched together on the short edges,
allowing a 3″ vent at the bottom to make it
easy to slip the finished camisole over the
head. Then the straps were stitched on.

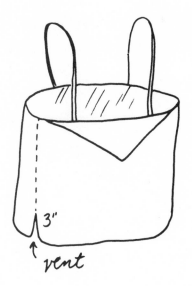

3″

vent

HANKY
CAMISOLE

after

25¢

before

HANDWORK BODICE

A maize corduroy dress was found at a freestore. It had a raggedy bodice and long sleeves, but the skirt material was still in good shape.

1.

cut for straps

cut away here

2.

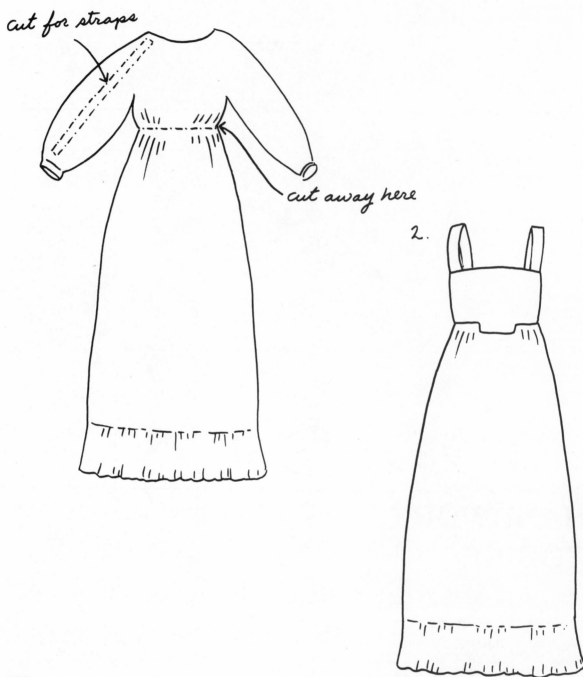

40¢

HANDWORK
BODICE

after

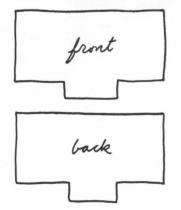

1. The bodice and sleeves were cut away.
2. Two identical hand-crocheted pieces (found at a thrift shop for forty cents) were sewn together front and back as a bodice. These were attached to the skirt.

67

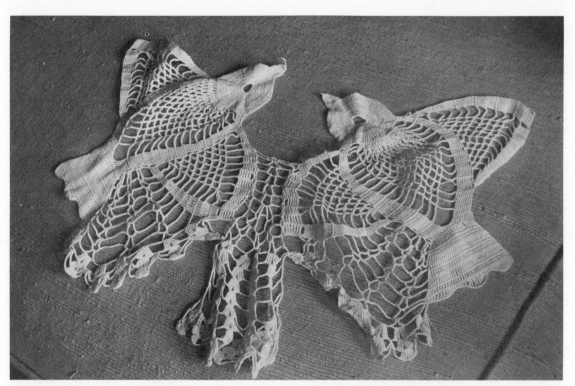

before

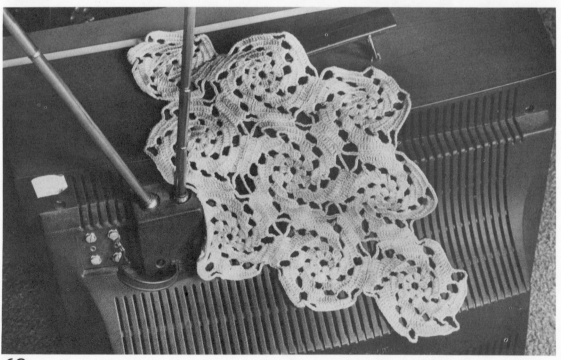

68

DAINTY DOILIE DOLLIES

after

Nona (at right) is an inveterate collector. Her greatest moment was when she and a friend found a truck full of clothes at the dump. Nona stepped back, not wanting to be greedy, and the friend got the best of the lot. "Taught me not to hesitate," she says. Now she digs right in.

The birds cost fifty cents and the rainbow-colored doilie was a quarter. The head parts of the birds were stitched to the straps of the man's undershirt. The rainbow (on Barcat, behind kaleidoscope) was sewn (around the edge) to a simple muslin halter.

69

before

ONE DOZEN LACE COASTERS

In the days of refined living, well before paper towels, these antique coasters held highballs on mahogany table tops. Now a new use has shown up for them. Here, six were appliquéd to each sleeve of this black T-shirt dress.

Here's a little secret: Hand stitch with a little give, so that when the T-shirt material stretches out, the lace will lay flat against your body. You may not always find lace coasters, but linen ones are just as nice.

70

$3

after

before

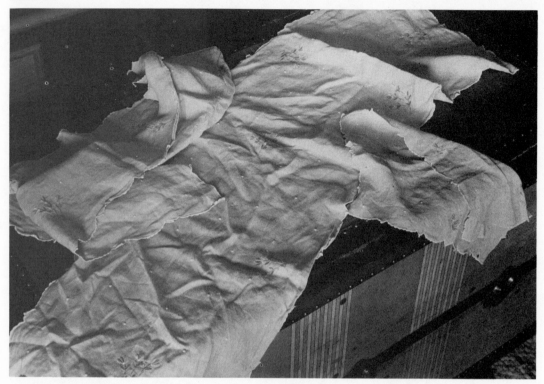

DRESSER SCARF DRESS

The dresser scarf was an absolute necessity on every table, bureau . . . and dresser. Of course they were decorative, usually combining embroidery with lace, but they were also practical protection for natural wood surfaces.

"This is for the more advanced recycler," says Shahastra, "because you have to figure it out as you go along, like a little puzzle." The dresser scarves cost three dollars. The fabric cost another two.

1. There were three scarves, two measuring 33" by 16" and one small one about 8" square.
2. Two panels measuring about 6" on top and expanding to 12" on the bottom were cut for the sides.

72

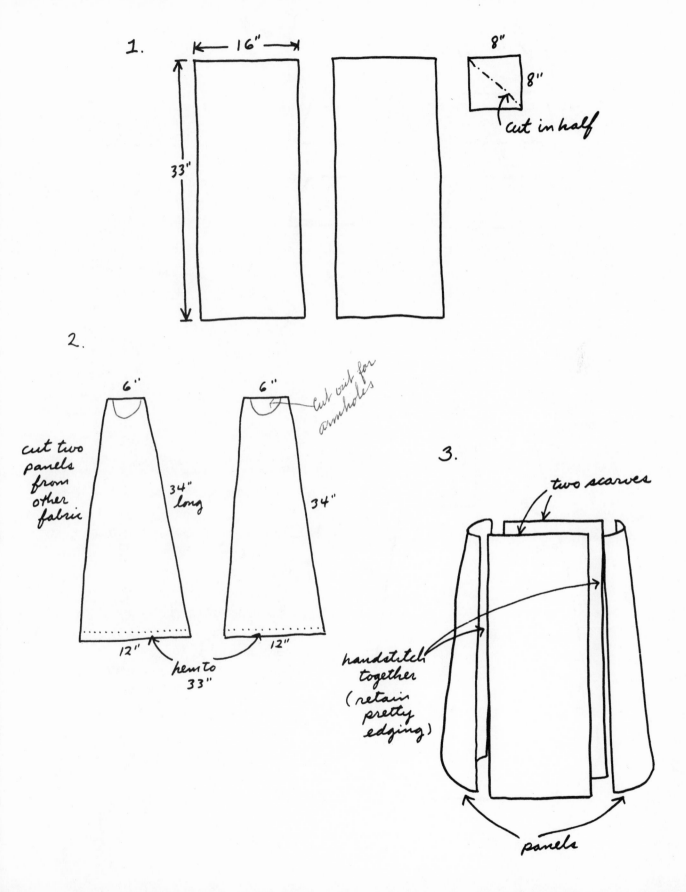

1.

16"

33"

8"

8"

cut in half

2.

6"

cut two panels from other fabric

34" long

6"

Cut out for armholes

34"

12"

12"

hem to 33"

3.

two scarves

handstitch together (retain pretty edging)

panels

4. cut 4 pieces

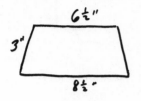
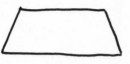

6½"

3"

8½"

5.

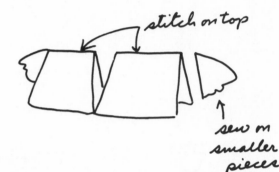

stitch on top

sew on smaller pieces

6.

sew to bottom

3. Since the scarves had a pretty edging detail, they were hand stitched to the panels.

4. Then two pieces for the front yoke and two for the back, each measuring 3″ × 6″ × 8″, were cut out. (These will have to be cut to fit your own measurements and neckline style, and also to fit the dresser scarves you are working with.)

5. The yoke pieces were sewn to the top of the dresser scarves, so they fit exactly to the outer edges, front and back. Diagonally-cut pieces from the third scarf were sewn into the top of the armhole at the shoulder to make the cap sleeves.

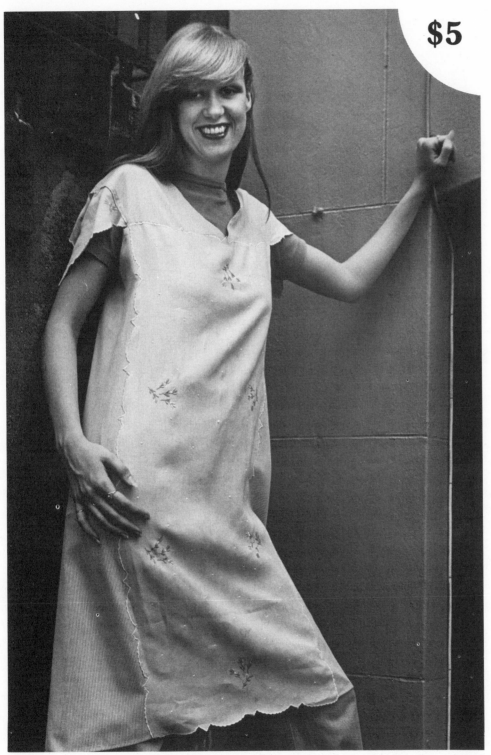

$5 DRESSER SCARF DRESS

after

75

before

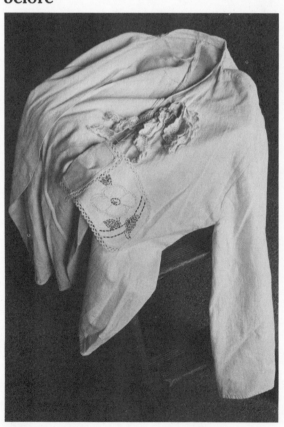

Antimacassars

Grandma put them on the backs and arms of sofas to keep hair oil off. But then hair oil went out of fashion and these anti-macassars found their way to the storage chest. Nowadays they can be bought cheap and used in a variety of inventive ways.

FANCY POCKET

Here, a pair of antimacassars was sewn to a muslin jacket to make pockets. The ironed-down top parts became pocket flaps. "Found" lace edging was stitched around the sleeve edges. (A baby pinafore is made from two antimacassars on page 122.)

FREE

after

Wearing the Drapes

Drapes are often made of sturdy, colorful, and imaginative recyclable fabrics. And, when they're castaways lurking about in some dusty old thrift shop bin, they'll cost you mere pennies. Think of them as yards and yards of fabric—with timeworn character.

There's such a joy in making a terrific new sun dress from a great old-timey flowered chintz drape, or a colorful caftan from white drapes dyed whatever shade you want. (A child's summer coat is made from café curtains on page 112.)

There's romance in it all. Not only that, my dear, there's practicality.

BARCAT'S DRAPE DRESS

The old drapes were in a bin at a thrift shop. The price was thirty cents. The pink flowers on the white chintz ground cried out to be sewn into a summer dress. Barcat removed the pleats from the top of the drapes and, using a standard sun dress pattern, whipped one up for herself. "I love making something out of nothing," she says.

30¢

after

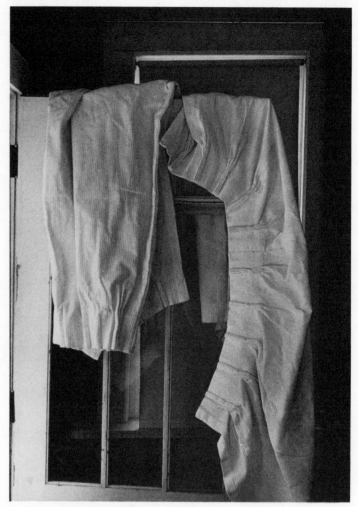

A CAFTAN FOR ZUBIN

Here, Zubin wears wife Shahastra's concoction from old drapes. Baby Zandra hangs in there. Shahastra bought the two big white corded drapes for seventy-five cents. After taking the tucks off the top, she washed the drapes. Then using dye you can find at supermarkets and dime-

stores, she dyed one fuchsia, one gold. The quality of the fabric made the colors come out pastels. Then, using a standard commercial caftan pattern that had four panels as a basic body, she laid out the dyed drapes, alternating colors on the sleeves and the caftan bottom.

80

after

Bedspreads and Blankets: Off the Bed and On Your Back

Just as drapes make handsome clothing material, so do bedspreads and blankets (sheets, too). And you'll even find (on page 118) that a pillow slip recycles into a child's dress.

You'll learn to make a dramatic coat from a raggedy chenille bedspread, a skirt from a flouncy flowered one, and a winter poncho from a camp blanket and an old ski cap. Check the bunting on page 126 and Mom's boots, page 150, for more ways to recycle an old blanket.

BOBBIE PEARLMAN'S PEACOCK COAT

Color Plate 12

It draws gasps when Bobbie walks by in it. It's her priceless possession, yet the old chenille bedspread from which it was made cost her only fifty cents. "It was torn so it was sold as a rag," says Bobbie. "Most people didn't know what could be done with it. But when I saw that peacock, I knew." The coat was made with a standard commercial pattern. (The simpler the better; this one had no collar, cuffs, or buttons.) "The inside had a nice finish, so I didn't have to line it," says Bobbie.

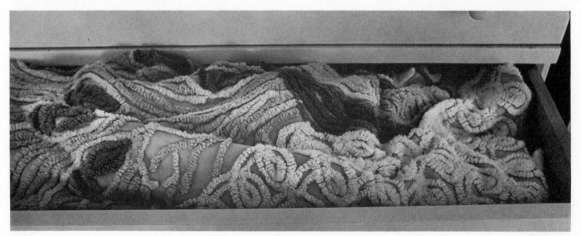

before

50¢

after

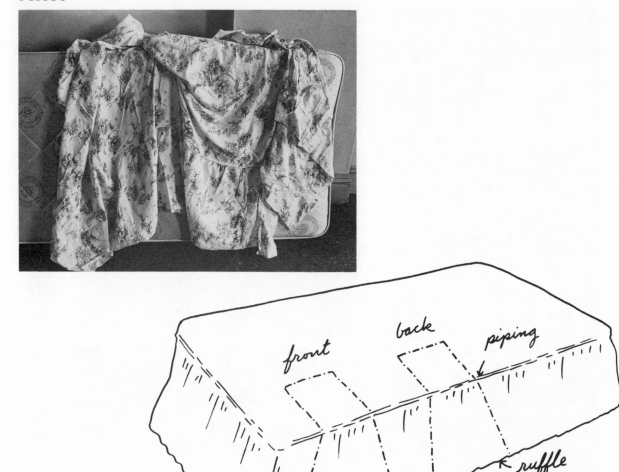

AND HARRIET'S BEDSPREAD SKIRT

Harriet found the bedspread in one of her forays and quickly turned it into a skirt.

"I took another skirt I owned and liked and laid it down on the bedspread, utilizing the flounce at the bottom. Then I cut out a new skirt, leaving an inch or two on each side for seams. Next, I pinned the two skirt pieces together and sewed up the sides. Last, I turned the waistline under to make a casing, then ran an elastic through it to fit. So simple, it was made in minutes."

84

FREE

after

before

NONA'S WINTER BLANKET

The heavy wool navy blue camp blanket used to be on Nona's bed. But one day she removed it, cut a hole in the middle, sewed an old ski hat (from a friend) around it—and pulled it over her head. She's worn it for three winters now.

FREE

after

2

FOR KIDS: HANDSOME HAND-ME-DOWNS

They grow so fast, kids do. No sooner have you outfitted them than it's time to do it again. Stretching the dollar can be a problem, whether you've got one youngster or a parcel of them.

One way to fill in the clothing gaps is to recycle old things into new ones for your babies and growing boys and girls. Terrific practically new clothes—sturdy rompers, T-shirts, sweaters, jackets—can often be bought worn *as is* from secondhand clothing stores.

But grownup garments can be creatively cut down for kids, too. Here, you'll find Daddy's shirt (in good strong cotton) made into Daughter's sun dress. Mom's favorite corduroy mini makes a zowie jumper, and a petticoat, pillow slip, and doilie turn into dresses.

There's more: a café curtain coat, an antimacasser pinafore, a blanket bunting, and a slicker colorfully done up with plastic tapes. And in the "Color Me" section beginning on page 163, you'll learn to use waterproof markers and crayons to spruce up your child's clothes.

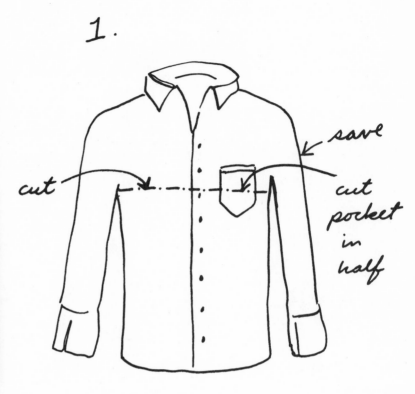

DADDY'S SHIRT

The shirt belonged to Dejha's father. It was a crisp striped one hundred percent cotton. Little girls' dresses in such nice fabric cost a pretty penny. But Mommy's friend Jane MacLeod Pappidas, a children's wear designer, is a resourceful lady. She whipped up a sun dress for Dejha, and it didn't cost a cent. "The dress took only an hour to make," says Jane, "and you couldn't find a lovelier fabric, or a cheaper one. It's hard to get beautiful cottons these days. When you find a good cotton like the one in this

shirt, you should keep it circulating." If Dejha looks unhappy in the picture on page 92, it isn't that she doesn't like her snappy sun dress. She's not at all sure she likes having her picture taken.

1. To make the sun dress, the shirt was cut across the body right below the sleeves through the pocket, retaining half of it (or it could be removed), and through the side seams and the shirt's front placket with buttons.

89

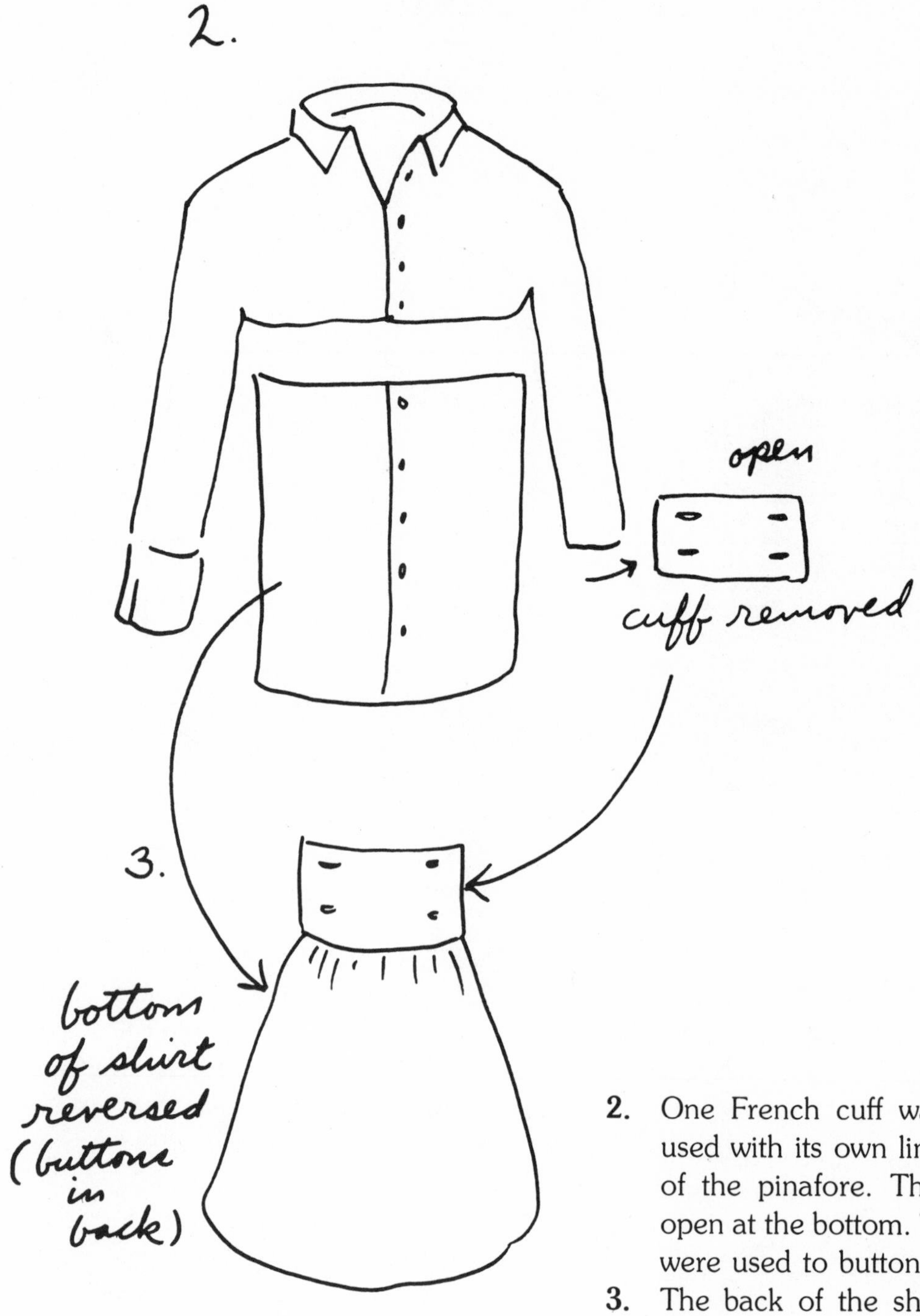

2.

open

cuff removed

3.

bottom
of shirt
reversed
(buttons
in
back)

2. One French cuff was removed and used with its own lining for the front of the pinafore. The cuff was now open at the bottom. The cuff-link slits were used to button on the straps.

3. The back of the shirt was gathered and sewn to the pinafore front, matching the side seams to the edges of the cuff.

4.

back

straps
made
from
shirtsleeves

4. The front shirt placket was retained to button the dress up the back. At the waist, elastic was added so that it would hug the child's back. Straps made from the sleeves were sewn to the sun dress back. Buttons were sewn on the other ends and the straps were then crisscrossed and fastened to the buttonholes at the pinafore front. The garment was then hemmed and Dejha's name embroidered on the yoke. The apron was made from a hand-crocheted table mat found at a thrift shop for ten cents.

91

after

10¢

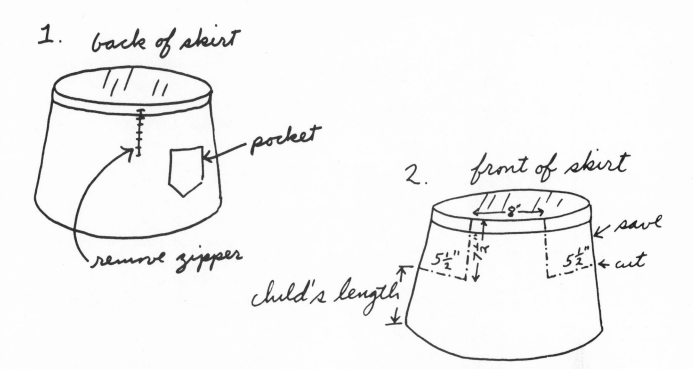

1. *back of skirt*

pocket

remove zipper

2. *front of skirt*

8"

7½"

5½"   *save*

5½"   *cut*

child's length

before

MOMMY'S MINI

Cheyenne's mommy Helen saves everything. She's even got a bunch of her old miniskirts. And thank goodness, because this short flowered one made a dandy four-year-old's jumper.

1. First, the zipper was removed from the miniskirt.
2. Then the skirt was laid out flat—the hem retained for the jumper. The child's length was measured from waist to hemline, and the top part of the skirt back cut off at this point. From here it was cut around the skirt to 5½″ beyond each side seam. Then straight up 7½″ and across 8″, a yoke was cut out.

93

3.

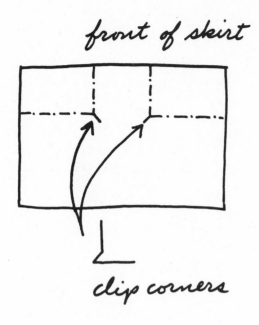

front of skirt

clip corners

3. A clip was cut $\frac{3}{4}''$ into each corner.
4. The skirt's pocket was removed and sewn to the yoke front. But before that was done, a 1″ ruffle (on the fold from a 2″ piece of any pretty cotton material) was attached under the pocket edge. (If there is no skirt pocket, one measuring $4'' \times 5''$ with a point at the bottom can be made from leftover skirt pieces.)
5. Next a yoke facing was cut and, right sides together, sewn to the front, allowing a $\frac{3}{4}''$ seam.
6. Then the yoke was turned to the outside and pressed.
7. Across the jumper back, right sides together, a $2\frac{1}{2}''$ facing was sewn.

4.

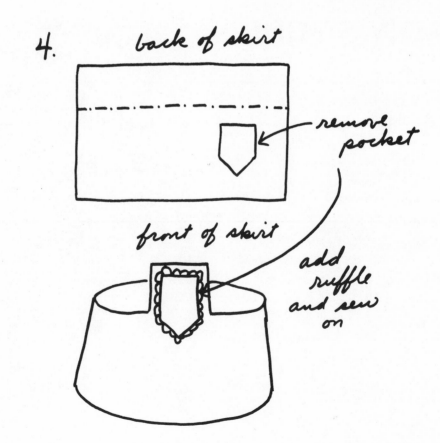

back of skirt

remove pocket

front of skirt

add ruffle and sew on

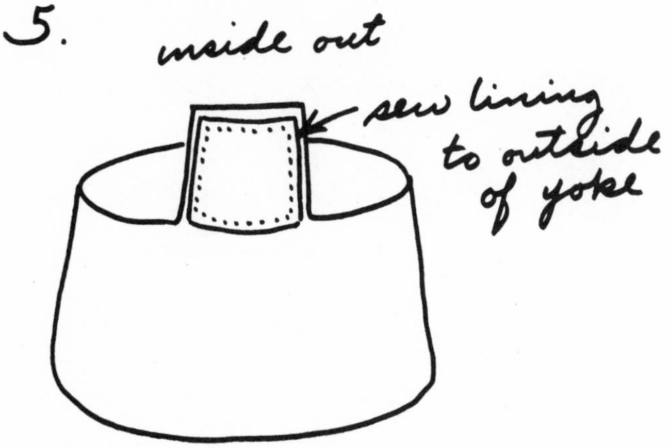

5. inside out

sew lining to outside of yoke

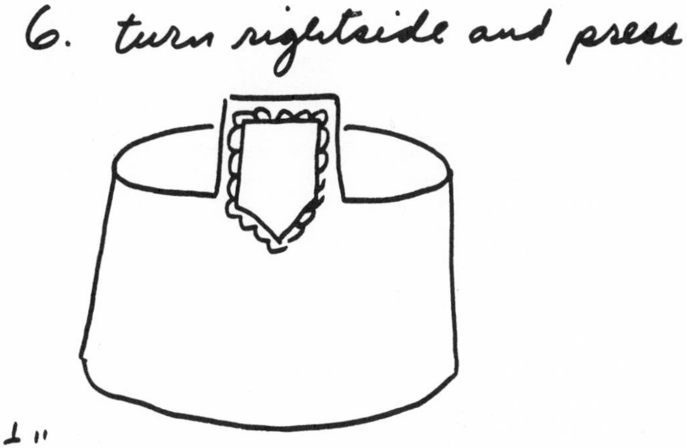

6. turn rightside and press

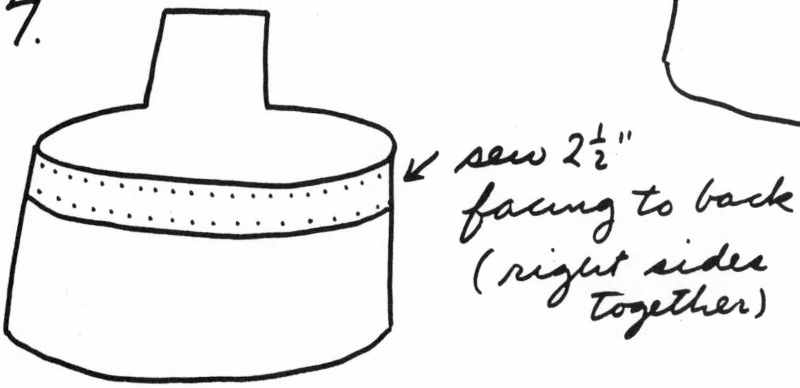

7. sew $2\frac{1}{2}$" facing to back (right sides together)

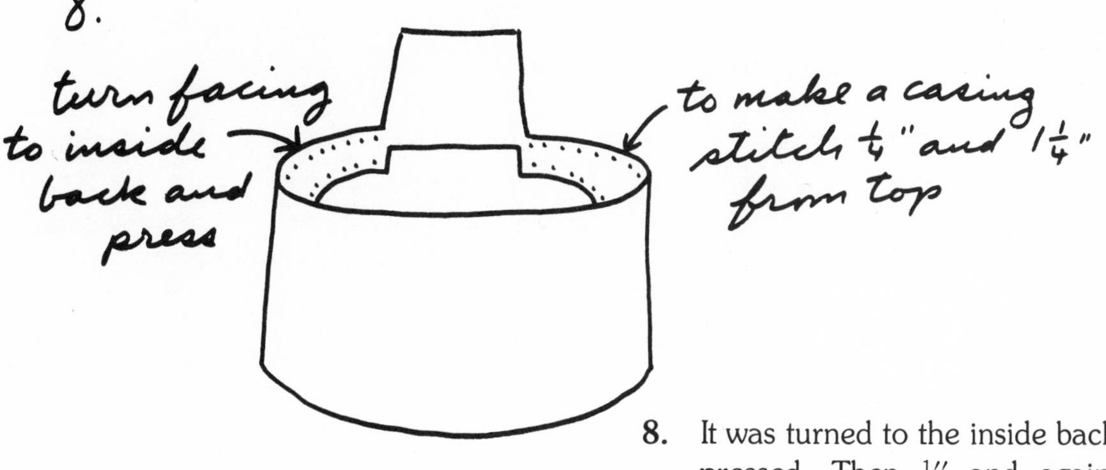

8. turn facing to inside back and press

to make a casing stitch $\frac{1}{4}$" and $1\frac{1}{4}$" from top

8. It was turned to the inside back and pressed. Then $\frac{1}{4}$" and again $1\frac{1}{4}$" down from the top edge it was stitched all around to make a 1" casing.

9.

draw $\frac{3}{4}$" elastic through casing

10.

9. Through the casing a $\frac{3}{4}$" elastic was drawn to make the jumper fit snugly across the child's back.

10. From the leftover miniskirt fabric, back pieces for straps were cut to fit the child's measurements. Then a facing cut from the same material as was used for the ruffle was sewn to the straps. They were attached to the back of the jumper, crisscrossed, and attached with industrial snaps to the yoke.

Color Plate 1
EIGHT
SCARVES

*For project
instructions,
see page 38.*

Color Plate 2
TWELVE
TIES

*For project
instructions,
see page 34.*

Color Plate 3
OLD STOCKING BAGS

*For project instructions,
see page 134.*

Color Plate 4
OLD NIGHTIE
WITH
NEW MEANING

*For project instructions,
see page 54.*

Color Plate 5
OLD COAT:
NEW CAP AND MITTENS

For project instructions, see page 130.

Color Plate 6
BLANKET BUNTING
AND MOM'S BOOTS

*For project instructions on bunting,
see page 126
and for Mom's boots,
see page 150.*

Color Plate 7
OLD LEATHER
AND NEW PAINT

*For project instructions,
see page 175.*

Color Plate 8
FROM ICK TO SLICK

*For project instructions,
see page 124.*

Color Plate 9
COLOR ME POLKA DOT

*For project instructions,
see page 167.*

Color Plate 10
LENS PINS

For project instructions, see page 160.

Color Plate 11
AIMEE'S PALETTE

*For project instructions,
see page 170.*

Color Plate 12
PEACOCK
COAT

*For project
instructions,
see page 82.*

DEJHA'S DOILIE DRESS

In all her four years, Dejha has not had such a pretty dress. Jane MacLeod Pappidas made it for her from a green and ecru bureau runner, bought at a thrift shop for twenty-five cents.

To the runner, a double crochet stitch was added to make the skirt. Six to eight stitches were added to each row to give the skirt flare. Then straps were crocheted to the top.

106

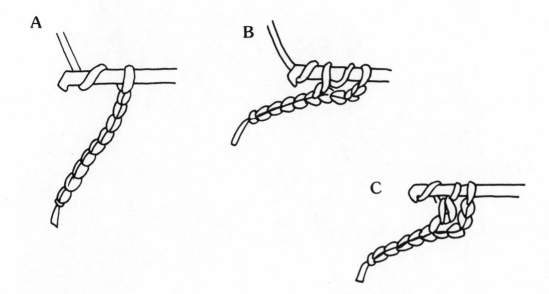

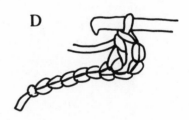

DOUBLE CROCHET

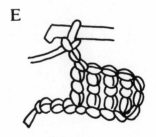

Begin with a slip knot on the hook. To chain, pass hook under yarn and catch with hook. Pull through loop. Continue for desired number of chain stitches (A). For double crochet stitch, yarn over hook once and insert hook in fourth chain from hook. Yarn over hook (B) and pull through two loops on hook (C). Yarn over and pull through last two loops on hook. You will now have one loop on hook (D). Continue across chain (E). To turn at end of each row, chain two. To add stitches as you go (known as increasing), work two double crochet stitches in one stitch . . . a one stitch increase.

107

**DEJHA'S
DOILIE
DRESS**
after

25¢

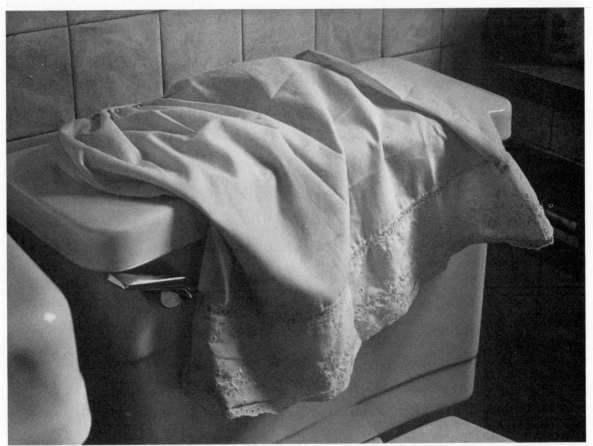

MAMA'S PETTICOAT

The pink dacron petticoat belonged to Cheyenne's mother. She had no use for the petticoat anymore, but saw a little girl's pinafore rising up out of the nice machine-embroidery edging. She snipped, clipped, and sewed, and came out with a pretty thing for her daughter.

To make the pinafore, Helen first cut

109

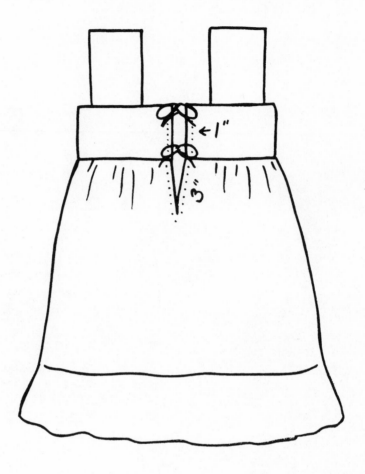

the elastic off the top of the half-slip. She made a 3″ slit in the back (so that the dress would be easy for the child to get over her head). Then she hemstitched it. The pinafore yoke was made from pink batiste blanket binding, measured to fit around Cheyenne with a 1″ seam allowance for the back opening. The ends of the binding were stitched back $\frac{1}{2}$″ on either side. The petticoat was gathered to the yoke, starting at one side of the hemmed slit and ending at the other. Two ribbon ties for fasteners were sewn to either side of the back yoke opening. Straps made from the same binding were measured to fit the shoulder, then sewn to the yoke.

110

FREE MAMA'S PETTICOAT

after

111

before

CAFÉ CURTAIN COAT

Jane MacLeod Pappidas found this curtain at Goodwill Industries for twenty cents. The pink gingham edging and the hearts in each corner intrigued her. She knew there was something there for a little girl. So she played around with the curtain for a while, until she found it.

112

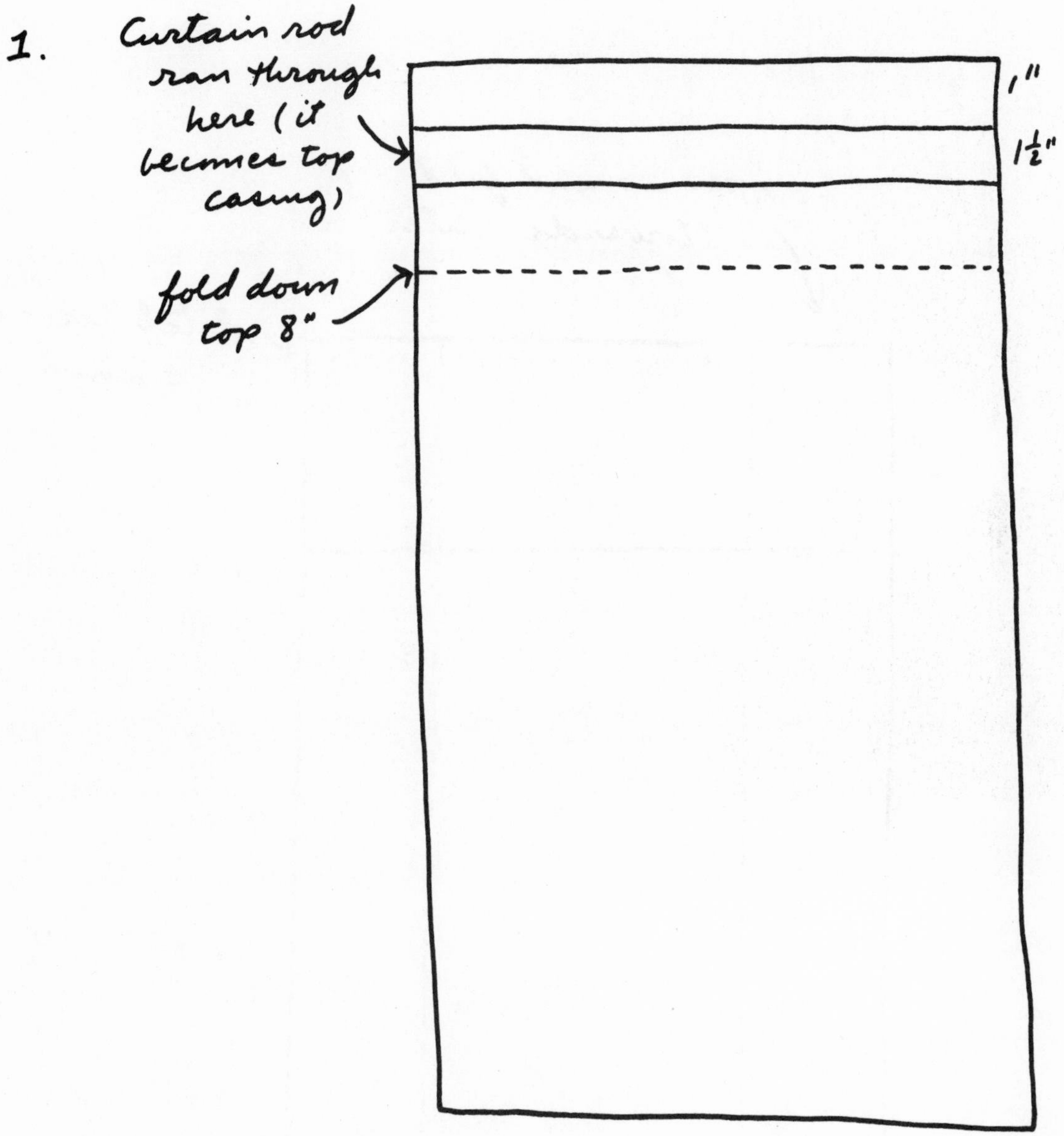

1. Curtain rod ran through here (it becomes top casing)

1"

1½"

fold down top 8"

1. The natural casings, through which the curtain rods had originally been drawn, gave her a clue. And soon a child's coat emerged.

113

2.

open up and fold
towards center

stitch across
½ down

8"

3.

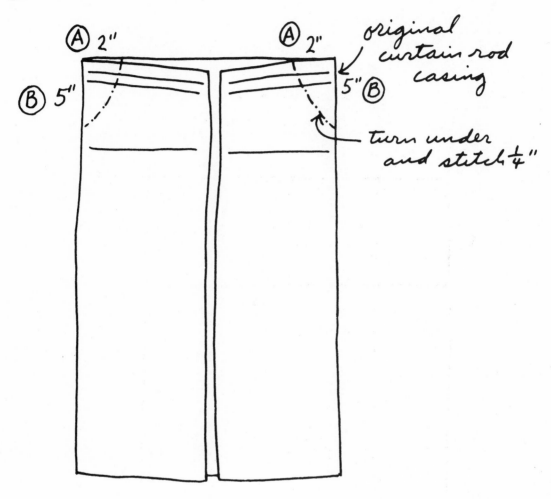

A 2"
A 2"   *original curtain rod casing*

B 5"
5" B

turn under and stitch ¼"

2. To make a second casing, the curtain was turned down 8″ at the top, and stitched 1½″ from the fold.

3. The two sides of the curtain were brought around to meet at the center. Then 2″ in from each side (A), and 5″ down (B), two armholes were cut and hemmed ¼″ from the edge.

115

4.

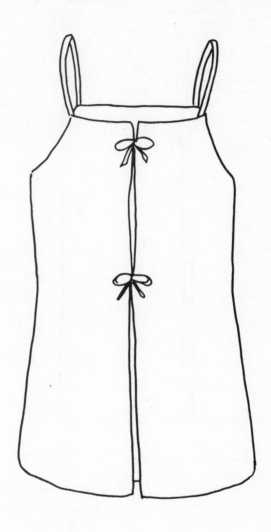

4. Last, two cords were drawn, one through the original curtain rod casing, the other through the newly made casing, and tied.

20¢ CAFÉ
CURTAIN
COAT

after

117

before

SAVITRI'S PILLOW SLIP DRESS

The red, white, and blue stripes were just made for a kid. The pillow slip lay on a Goodwill Industries' counter, waiting for a mother to recognize its worth. The price was thirty cents. Cheyenne's mommy Helen bought it for Cheyenne's friend Savitri. It was to be a birthday present. And did she love it? Yes, she did. Just look at her swing in it on page 121.

1. There was too much red at the edge of the pillow slip, so Helen cut off half of it to use for trimmings and bindings.
2. Then she turned under a $\frac{1}{4}''$ hem and machine stitched it up. At the other end, she cut the pillow slip off at a point where it would measure the right length for Savitri from shoulder to hemline (17" for her).
3. Then she folded the pillow slip piece lengthwise. Four inches down from raw edge (A) and $2\frac{1}{2}''$ in (B) she penciled in a curve, leaving $1\frac{1}{2}''$ at the top. Then she cut through four thicknesses along the pencil line.

118

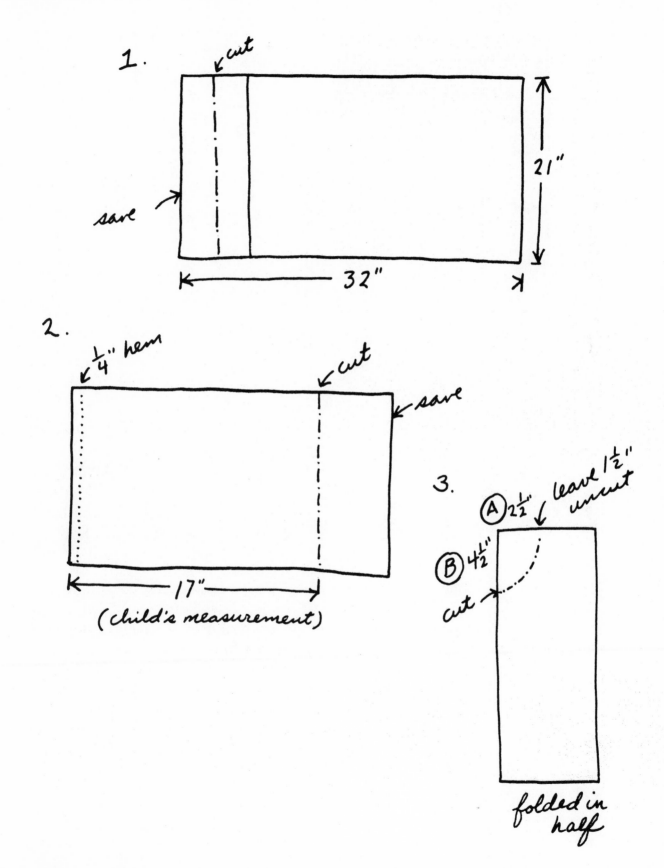

1.

cut

save

21"

32"

2.

¼" hem

cut

save

17"

(child's measurement)

3.

Ⓐ 2½"   leave 1½" uncut

Ⓑ 4½"

cut

folded in half

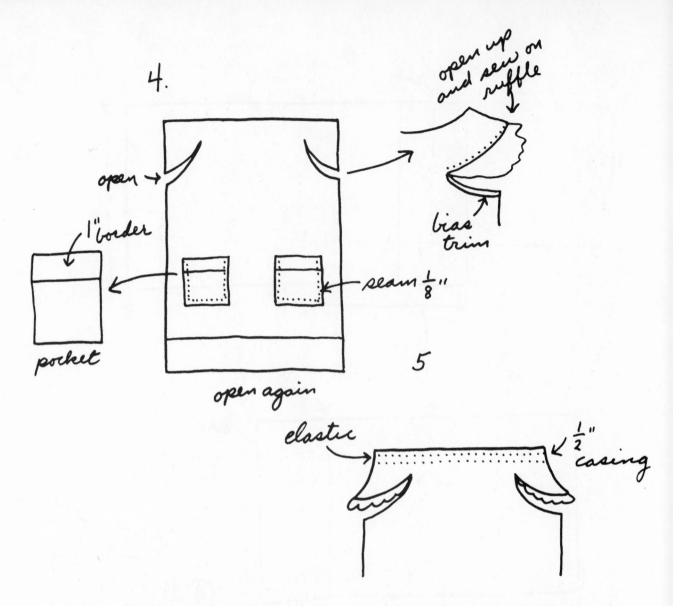

4. Now, unfolding the pillow slip, she spread the curves apart and sewed a $\frac{1}{4}''$ red bias binding to the lower edge on each side. (The binding was cut from the leftover red material.) A 2″-wide ruffle was cut from a double piece of red and sewn to the top of the curve on either side. Patch pockets $4\frac{1}{4}'' \times 3\frac{1}{4}''$ were cut from the leftover striped material so that the pocket stripes were perpendicular to the dress stripes. A 1″ border was sewn to the pocket tops before they were topstitched to the dress.

5. A small opening was left at the center back to pull $\frac{1}{2}''$ elastic through with a safety pin. The elastic was pulled tight enough to fit Savitri snugly on top. Then the elastic was stitched across the end to keep it in place.

120

SAVITRI'S
PILLOW SLIP
DRESS
after

before

ANTIMACASSER PINAFORE

Here's how to quickly doll up a diapered baby: Take two matching antimacassers. Attach ties at the shoulders and under the arms. Tie on the baby.

122

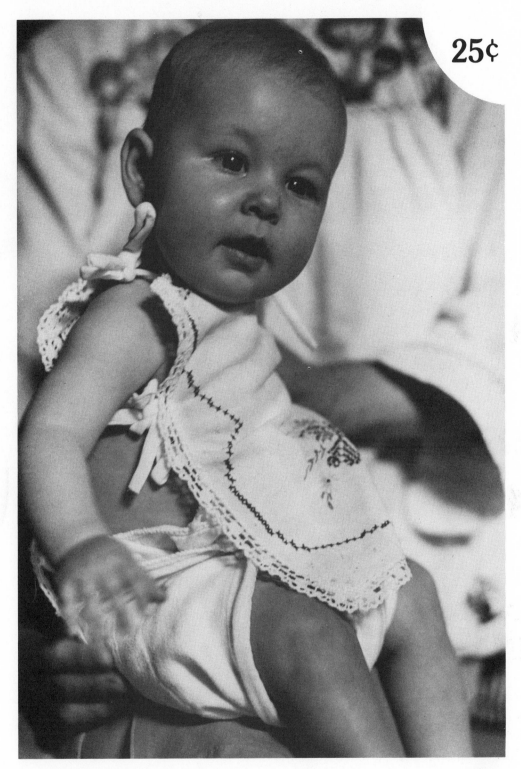

25¢

after

before

FROM ICK TO SLICK

Color Plate 8

It seemed that this slicker had had it. Here and there were snags and brown spots. But artists Rick and Glory Brightfield saw a swan in this ugly duckling. So they bought it for two dollars and turned it into a masterpiece of color and design. Glory took the back, Rick the front, and they began taping pieces of plastic tape to it. Two rolls each of 1″ white, red, green, and blue tape were used, plus one roll each of $1\frac{1}{2}$″ blue, red, and green. The tapes were spread out on a flat cutting surface. Then, using a single-edged razor-blade, they cut them into rectangles and squares, none bigger than $1\frac{1}{2}$″. This way several colors could be picked up as the design began to grow. A geometric design worked best. The tape was sealed down with their fingers as they went along. "Occasionally, pieces have come loose at the edges, and our daughter Savitri picked them off," says Rick. "So we've just cut off another square and replaced the vacant spot."

124

after

50¢

ZANDRA'S BLANKET BUNTING

Color Plate 6

Mommy Shahastra found a twin-size red blanket at Goodwill Industries for fifty cents. A baby layette pattern, which included a bunting, was used. Three different colored trims (red, purple, and blue) were sewn down the front. The blue was used around the hood and sleeve. Shahastra's boots were made from the rest of the blanket. See page 150 for instructions on making the boots.

126

3

EVERYTHING THAT ISN'T PANTS, SKIRTS, COATS, AND DRESSES

Here's the kit and caboodle, all the zany and pretty things to recycle from odds and ends found here and there.

Start with a sweater or an old coat and end up making it into mittens. Turn stocking bags into shoulder bags, a hand-hooked rug into a carpet bag, a well-worn knapsack into a wonder of patchwork femininity.

Let buttons and old drapery fringe, discarded eyeglasses, or travel souvenirs become jewelry. Sew solid gold watch parts to a vest pocket. Convert your worn blue jeans into a hat. Search for antique buckles and ribbons to make up a belt. End up with a collection of accessories that will be the envy of all the girls on the block.

127

before

SWEATER MITTENS

The magenta sweater cost twenty-five cents at a thrift shop. The royal blue doilies were a dime for two. Most likely you won't find doilies to duplicate the ones used here. But any number of decorative details could be used.

The mittens were made by tracing a pattern around each hand onto brown paper. Then the paper patterns were cut out and pinned to the sweater, using the lower ribbed edge as the wristband. The sweater front and back made up the double mitten pieces. Before the front and back were sewn together, a doilie was pinned to each of the two mitten front pieces and stitched. Beads were sewn up the front of each doilie. Finally, the right sides of the mittens were sewn together. Then the mittens were turned right side out.

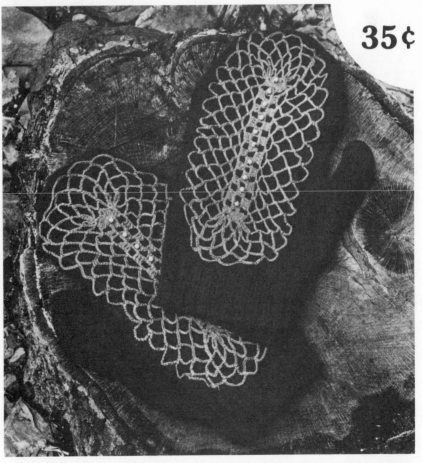

after

OLD COAT: NEW CAP AND MITTENS

Color Plate 5

The coat, a white wool fleece, cost seventy-five cents at a thrift shop. The hat and mittens were cut from the back of the coat.

1. The scalloped detail was utilized, and the coat hem cut out "soldier hat" fashion. The hat measured 12"—half the head's circumference (in this instance 22")—by a crown depth of $8\frac{1}{2}$".
2. Right sides together, it was stitched all around, leaving a $\frac{1}{2}$" seam.
3. Little slashes were cut at intervals, so that the seam would turn smoothly. The hat was turned to the right side and embroidery added-satin and stem stitch, French knots, lazy daisy stitch. See pages 186 and 187 for instructions. The mittens were made the same way as from the sweater, except that these were machine hemmed. And, if you wish to add bulk, a baby's crib pad does fine (the one used here was five cents from a thrift shop) and can be cut to the shape of the mittens for a lining.

130

1.

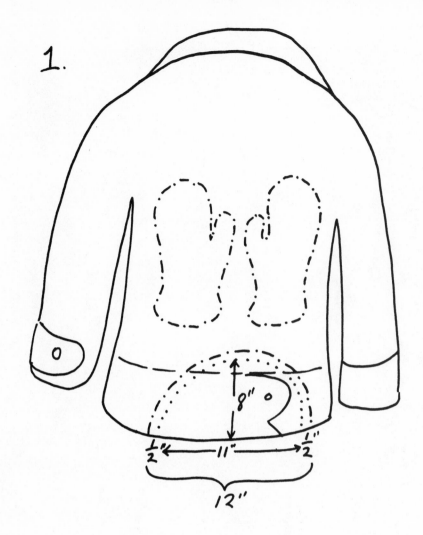

8"

½" ← 11" → ½"

12"

2.

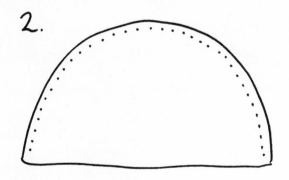

3.

clip seams

OLD COAT:
NEW CAP
AND
MITTENS
after

80¢

PATCHWORK PACK

First the bag sprang a little rip, which was patched. That patch looked so terrific that one followed another. Until—well, here you have it.

before

134

OLD
STOCKING BAGS
Color Plate 3

Everyone used to have them in the days
before bare legs, blue jeans, and trousers.
Now you can pick them up in thrift shops.
I bought these two (at left) for one dollar
each. I've also paid three dollars and five
dollars for them. Never found my name
on one—only Ellen's.

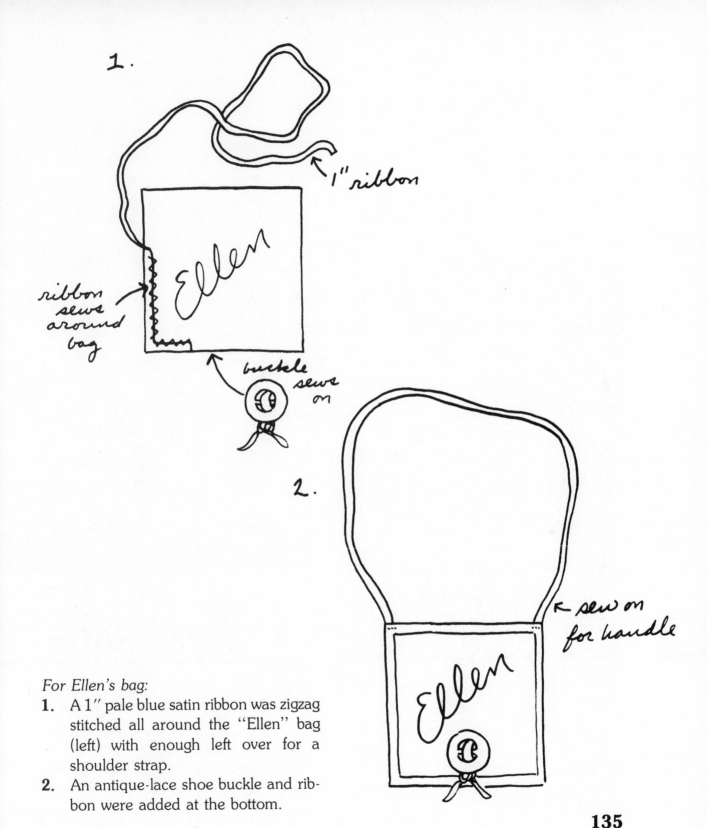

1.

1" ribbon

ribbon sews around bag

buckle sews on

2.

← sew on for handle

For Ellen's bag:

1. A 1″ pale blue satin ribbon was zigzag stitched all around the "Ellen" bag (left) with enough left over for a shoulder strap.
2. An antique-lace shoe buckle and ribbon were added at the bottom.

135

1.

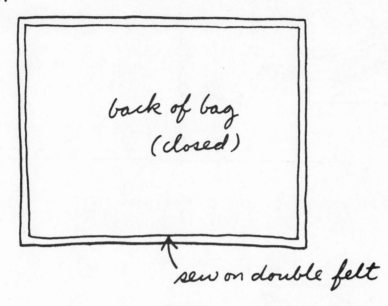

back of bag
(closed)

sew on double felt

2.

front of bag
(open
  inside)

sew double

3.

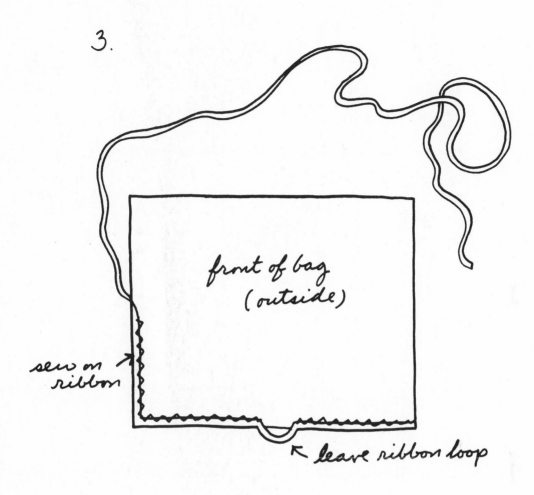

front of bag
(outside)

sew on ribbon →

← leave ribbon loop

The other bag:

1. A double layer of felt for weight was zigzag stitched to the back of the other bag (at right).
2. And double felt was zigzag stitched to the inside to make a pocket.
3. The top flap of the bag was edged with 1″ polka dotted grosgrain ribbon. A small ribbon loop was left at the bottom to fasten an antique button (sewn on last).

137

4.

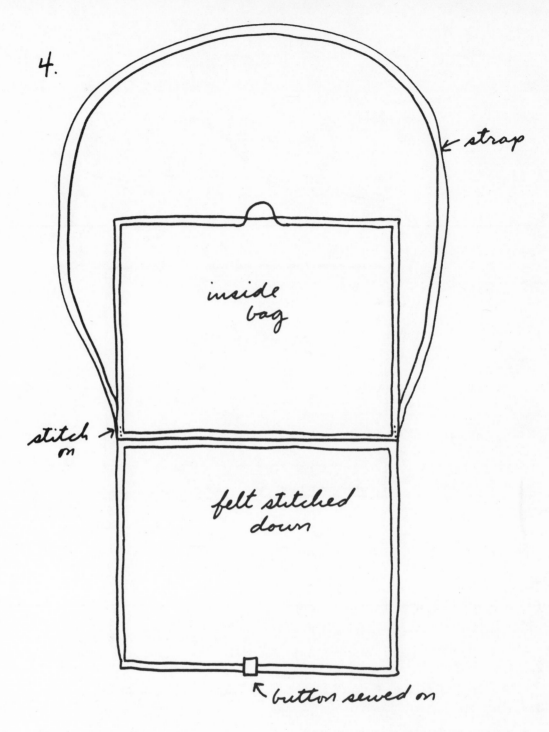

The same 1″ grosgrain ribbon was backed with a heavier velvet ribbon to make a shoulder strap. Then it was folded down the middle and stitched again to make the strap strong. Finally, it was stitched to the back side of the bag under the lace side of the flap, and the antique button sewn on.

before

MICHAEL'S CARPET BAG

Someone put precious time into hand hooking this old rug. But there it lay in a Goodwill Industries store, tired looking and dirty, with a five dollar price tag on it. Then Michael found the rug and put new life into it as a carpet bag. "Old materials have more appeal for me," says Michael. "Like old silver has a lovely patina, so does the surface of all cloth develop its own look. It was a past tied up with other lives and energies. I thought of the person who had patiently made the rug and of all the people who had passed over it.

"I used mild, cold-water soap to wash it and rug shampoo to lift up the nap," he says.

1.

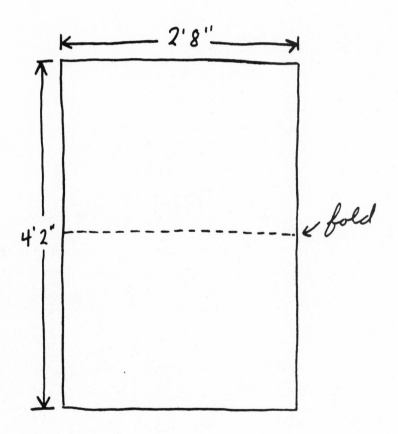

2'8"

4'2"

← fold

1. The rug measured 4'2" × 2'8". *50" × 32"* "Using a stitching awl, like the ones I'd used for leatherwork, I sewed it a little more than halfway up the sides."

141

2.

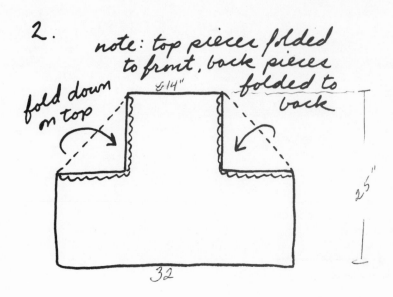

note: top pieces folded to front, back pieces folded to back

fold down on top

folded to back

≤ 14"

2⁵"

32

3.

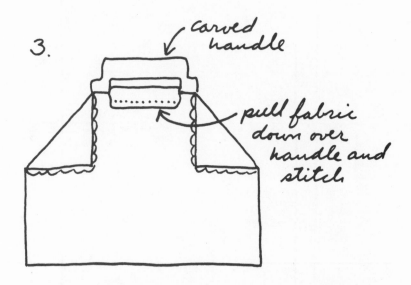

carved handle

pull fabric down over handle and stitch

2. "Then, at each of the four top corners, I sewed the bag over at a forty-five-degree angle, leaving a space of about 14″ for the wooden handles." (They were cut out with a saber saw, the edges rounded with a carving knife, then sanded down. Last, the **142** flower design was painted on it. The handle need not be this complicated. Wooden dowels could be used, or old suitcase handles.)

3. The top of the carpet bag was looped over the handle on either side and stitched down.

$5

MICHAEL'S
CARPET BAG

after

If those corners & top edges were folded to inside, they'd make "pockets" & leave design of rug less marred.

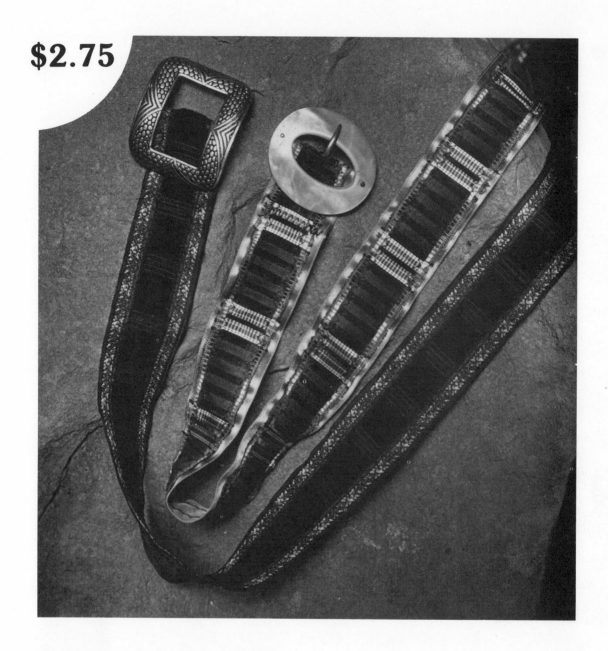

$2.75

RIBBON BELTS

The ribbons used for these belts are vintage 1870, costing seventy-five cents each at an antique store. The mother-of-pearl and the steel Twenties buckles cost two dollars each at another antique store. Each belt took five minutes to make. Stiffer ribbons were used for backings; then buckles were attached.

144

JONI'S JEANS CAP

Joni Minter loves her jeans. "I've lived in them since I was a twelve-year-old kid in Maryland," she says. "When my husband Lew [in picture] and I moved to New York, we were so poor I couldn't afford clothes. But I had a million pairs of blue jeans, so I started turning them into vests, skirts, and hats. Then I began to make and sell them to other people. I guess jeans are part of my whole trip in life."

145

1.

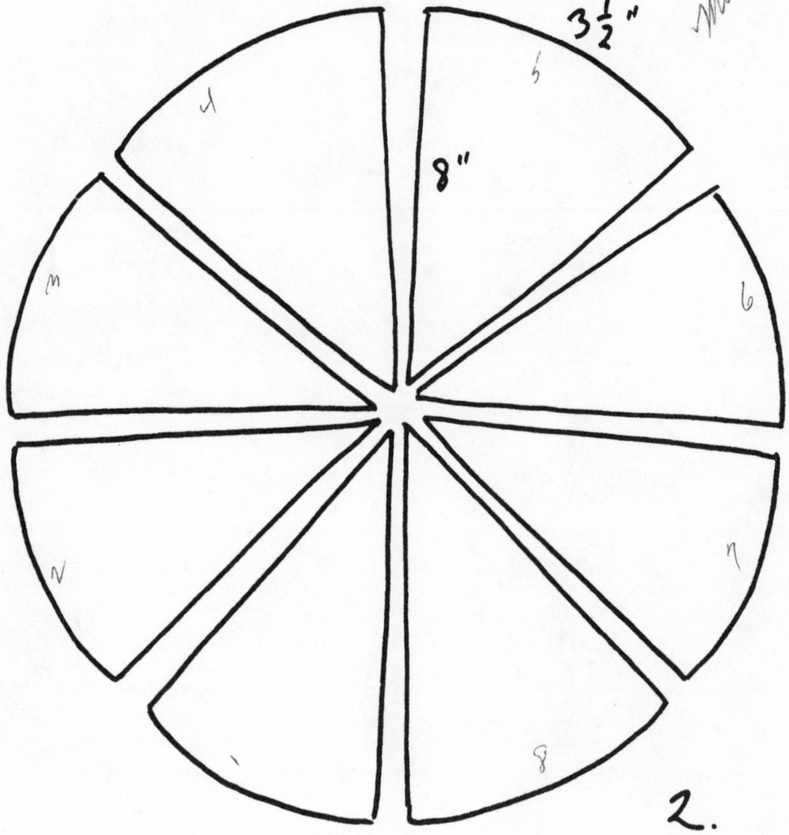

3½"

8"

2.

146

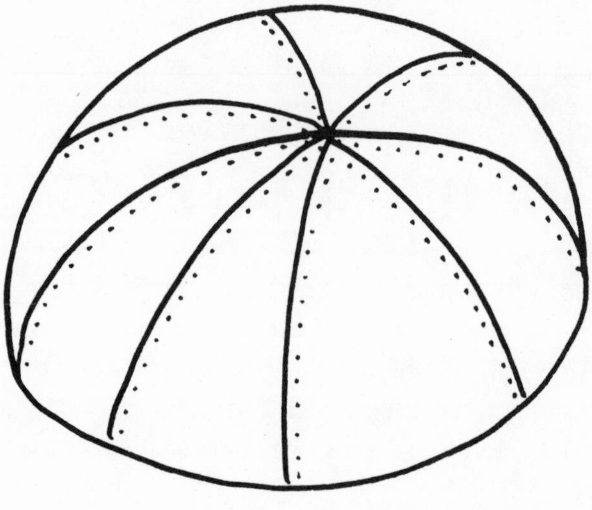

3.

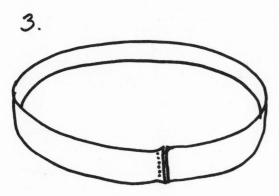

1. To make her jeans cap, Joni cut her jeans apart at the seams and laid the denim out flat to use as fabric. Then she made (in newspaper) an elongated oval spade pattern $3\frac{1}{2}''$ wide and 8″ long with a point at one end.

2. Eight denim sections were cut. Then, right sides together, she sewed one section to the other to form the cap shell. (You will find that they will match both at top and bottom.) The seam allowance was about $\frac{1}{2}''$. The seams were clipped so that they would curve smoothly when turned to the right side.

3. She measured her head with a tape measure, circling the brow. Then she added 1″ to her measurement for a seam allowance and seamed a $1\frac{1}{2}''$ strip of denim, which became the base that she sewed to the shell so it fit her head, blousing a little.

4. As the hat was a little too big at this point, she shirred one or two of the pie-like pieces with a running stitch.

4.

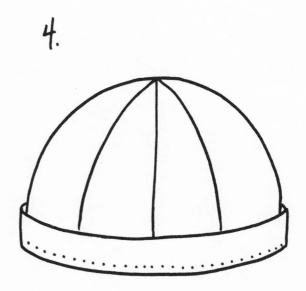

147

5.

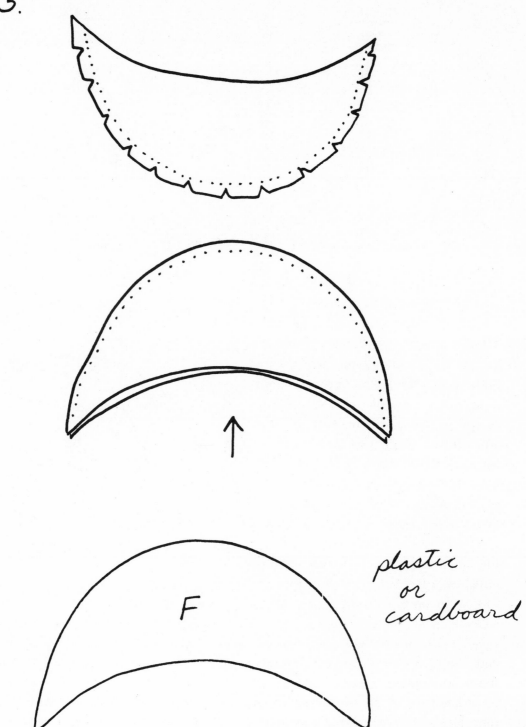

plastic
or
cardboard

F

148

6.

7.

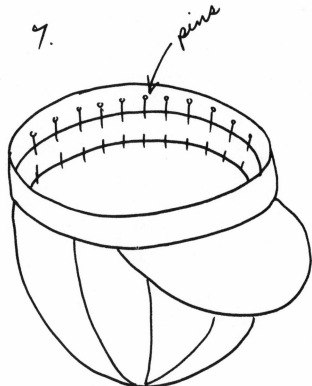

5. Then she cut two crescent-shaped pieces of denim which became the peak. Right sides together, she sewed them along the outside edges with $\frac{1}{4}''$ seams to make the cap's peak. Then she clipped the edges up to, but not through, the seams. This way they were smooth when she turned them to the other side. After turning the crescent shape to the right side, she pressed it and topstitched $\frac{1}{4}''$ in from the edge. Then she slipped a piece of cardboard (or plastic can be used) of the same shape inside the peak for stiffness (F).

6. For a lining, she cut a strip of satin 4″ wide and approximately 2″ longer than her head circumference. She sewed it to a circle of satin (10″ in diameter) and fit it inside the denim shell.

7. She pinned the shell, lining, and peak together, then placed a strip of grosgrain ribbon about $1\frac{1}{4}''$ wide to the right side of the denim along the edge and sewed it down. This served as a sweatband. Last, she sewed the four pieces together and turned the sweatband in.

149

MOM'S BOOTS

Color Plate 6

With the blanket fabric and blue trim left over from the baby bunting (page 126) Mommy made a pair of woolly indoor bootees for herself. They will keep feet warm on the coldest winter night.

1. First, she drew the size of her foot onto muslin. Then, using that for a pattern, she cut out a double sole for each foot.
2. For the tops, she cut two pattern pieces of what a silhouette of a boot would look like. She held these against her leg to see how close she was to getting the right shape. (If adjustments are to be made in the muslin pattern, they are made at this point.)
3. Then she cut the pieces out of the wool. Since they didn't allow enough room for the calf, she cut a triangular piece (first in muslin) to fit as a panel on the front of each leg. Then the bootee pieces were seamed together.
4. The ties, a yard long each—two for each bootee—were sewn on where the point of the triangular panel met the center seam at front. Then they were wrapped, ballet style, around the leg.

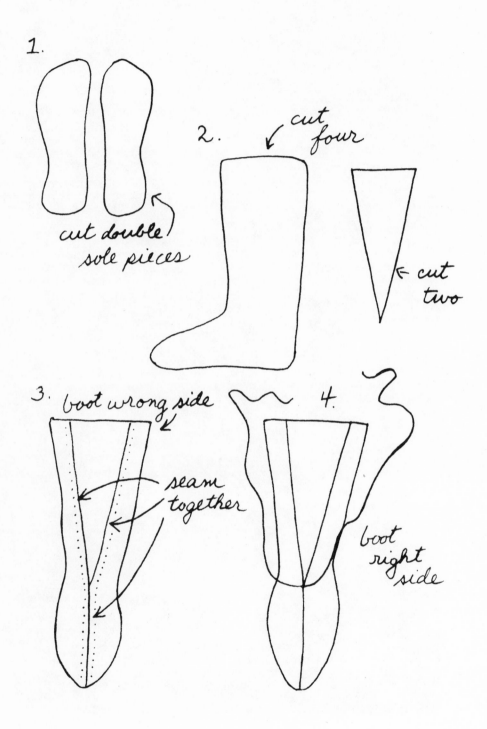

1.

cut double
sole pieces

2. cut four

cut two

3. boot wrong side

seam together

4. boot right side

50¢

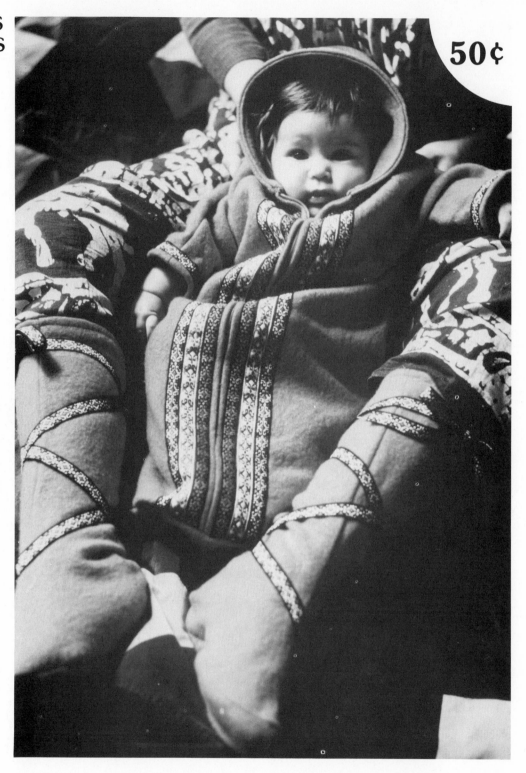

TUNA TIN AND OLD DENIM

Here, a tuna fish can was paired up with old denim to make a bracelet. Both ends were cut from the can and the rim was washed. Fabric was cut to fit the rim, allowing a $\frac{3}{4}''$ turnunder on both sides. Next, studs (about ten cents worth) were fastened to the denim and the studded denim was glued to the outside and inside edges of the can with white glue. A colorful striped ribbon (about twenty cents) was then glued over the raw edges with spray adhesive.

153

before

SOCKS THAT JINGLE, JANGLE, JINGLE

This project might really go in the category of making a silk purse out of a sow's ear. I was intrigued by the putty color of these old Army dress socks, which came all the way up to my knees (about twenty-five cents). So I poked around in my odds and ends collection, came up with a few shells, beads, and buttons, and strung

50¢

after

them to the cuff of the socks with silver thread (in all, about twenty-five cents). Then I did a little embroidery stitching, using green and red yarn. They have to be hand washed, which is a real pain in the neck, but the pleasure of wearing these jingle-jangle socks when I'm feeling silly is immeasurable.

THE WAYFARER'S NECKLACE

"My necklace is like a writer's journal," says Harriet. "It carries remembrances of a lot of things, people, places. It has been recycled many times. I take things off and put them back and make room for others. Practically everything had a hole in it already. If there wasn't one, I drilled it in with a jeweler's drill."

- Wooden beads from friends in California
- From my travels—a glass Eye of Fatima, worn for protection in the Middle East and Turkey
- A piece of flint found in the driveway of a house that I lived in when I was a little girl in England
- Glass beads from friends
- Old Afghan coins picked up in Afghanistan
- Teeth from a donkey, found on the Isle of Formentera
- My own wisdom tooth
- Tibetan amber from Nepal
- A polished stone from Nepal

- Vertebrae of small animals, found along the California coastal highway
- A shell from a California beach
- A seer stone from Moss Beach, California
- A cat's jaw, found in a parking lot in Bermuda
- A Tibetan coin with a hole in it
- An agate with a pine cone carved on it, from Afghanistan
- A horn of a goat, found in a ditch in Afghanistan
- A Tibetan hair parter made from a bird's claw
- A Mala prayer bead, given to me by an Indian holy man
- The neckbone of a bird, found in California
- A Tibetan coral bead from Nepal
- A mother-of-pearl bead from Nepal
- A Buddha's-eye bead from Tibet
- A wisdom tooth from a very good friend
- A coiled Ammonite, a fossil shell found in England on the beach at Lyme Regis

FREE

ART DECO BUTTONS

I have a cigar box where I throw old buttons. I've cut them off garments I no longer wear. I've bought secondhand clothes just for the buttons. I've been known to buy whole bottles of them for as much as ninety-nine cents. A couple of years ago, at an antique shop, I bought three art deco buttons for a nickle each. I've worn them as brooches, attaching them to my dress with a safety pin. Or I've pinned them to black satin ribbons and tied them around my wrist or neck. If the button hole is big enough, I've bobby-pinned them to my hair, or sewn then to grosgrain ribbons to make a belt or sash. They do wonders to dress up an old garment. I've just bought a dozen white rabbits, doubtless cut from a child's coat. And I'm building an outfit around ten art deco glass butterflies recently bought for one dollar. I've given old buttons as gifts. The uses are endless.

158

5¢

159

LENS PINS
Color Plate 10

Go to your optometrist and ask for his discarded lenses. Then make pins out of them. It's all so simple. One of these lens pins was made by gluing (with white glue) a wrapping-paper flower onto the back of the glass. (Any decorative paper that doesn't become transparent when wet will do.) A rainbow was painted onto the other pin, using glass paint. (Check your artists' supplies store for paint that adheres to glass.) Black or an opaque color painted on the lens back makes the design painted on the front show up more clearly. Last, glue a dime-store bar pin to the back.

160

HARRIET WITH A FRINGE

Silk fringe, the kind that used to be found on heavy velvet drapes in dark Victorian homes, made Harriet a dandy necklace when hung around her neck on a slender cord.

161

CLOCKWORK

Wornout clocks and watches have reusable parts. And sometimes these parts are gold. Here the real thing has been sewn onto a vest pocket.

162

4

COLOR ME

Think of clothes as canvas and draw or paint right on them. Markers and paints for doing this can be bought at your local art or crafts supplies store.

Crayon markers are among the newest materials. We jazzed up an ordinary blue and white polka dotted shirt with them (page 167). To heat set the colors and remove excess wax, paper was placed over the crayoned dots and the iron run over it.

Textile paints must also be heat treated to stay permanently on fabrics. Use the dryer to heat set textile-painted garments before washing them. To remove errors quickly, wash out the paint before throwing the clothes into the dryer.

Make sure that the unwaxed felt-tip markers are labelled *use on fabric* and *waterproof,* otherwise you can bet they'll not last through a first washing. Needlecraft markers have the best track record with most people. Aimee used these for her T-shirt (page 170).

Acrylics (water-based paints) can be thinned to any consistency needed for your design. (See the apple painted on Alex's shoulder, page 164.) Once dry, these paints are completely waterproof. (But note that cracking may occur if paint is put on too thickly.)

The materials used in this section were reasonably priced. A set of fifteen permanent crayon markers cost about $1.98. Felt-tip waterproof markers ran about $1.10 each. The acrylic paints were about .60 for a small tube and the textile paints about the same price for a small jar.

If you lack confidence as an artist, don't despair. You can trace designs onto cloth or leather and fill in the outlines with color (see page 175). Or, if you want, copy your designs from a magazine or book, using the grid method (page 200). Then again, you can brave it and express yourself freehand. There is a charm in simple, unprofessional-looking drawings. So don't be afraid. Just take off and do it.

163

ALEX'S PAINTED-ON T-SHIRTS

Paint on any old rag and make it come alive. Alex has dressed up two of her boyfriend's old T-shirts for herself. Use acrylic artists' paint that stay on no matter how many times you wash the shirt.

Regular dime-store stencils were used for her initials. With a felt-tip marker she drew their outlines through the stencil. Then she removed the stencil and filled in the outlines with a paintbrush.

164

To paint the apple or the flowers and pocket on your own T-shirts, trace the designs from this page using tracing paper. Then put carbon paper between the tracing and the T-shirt. Use an out-of-ink ballpoint pen to mark over the tracing, transferring the design to the T-shirt. Fill in the outline with paint.

165

ALEX'S
PAINTED-ON
T-SHIRTS
after

FREE

before

COLOR ME POLKA DOTS

Color Plate 9

1. This white polka dotted boy's shirt was found at a freestore.
2. Within minutes, Shahastra, a clothing designer, had cut off the collar. She multicolored the polka dots, using

167

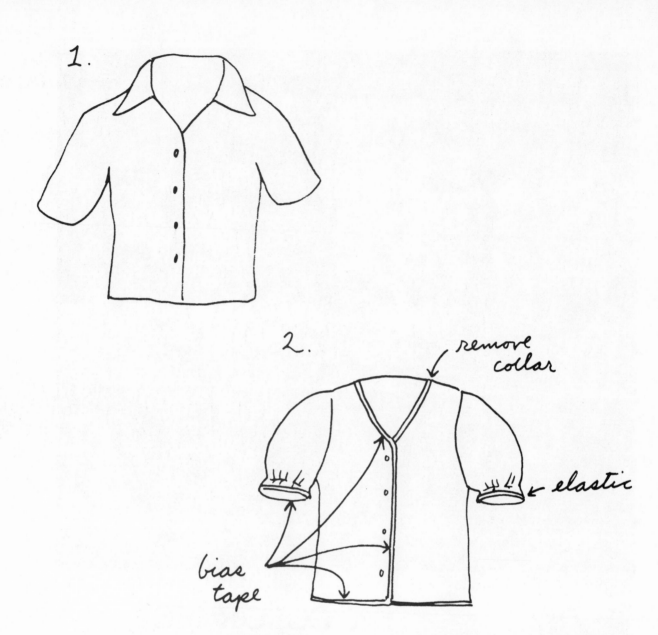

1.

2.

remove collar

elastic

bias tape

washable and ironable dyeing pastels. (Anything can be colored—stripes, squares, etcetera.) A piece of plain paper was placed over the colored polka dots and an iron run over them to heat set the colors. After that, she edged the entire shirt in bias tape, then puffed up the sleeves by sewing narrow elastic inside them about 1″ from the edge, so they fit the arms snugly. "I really like working on the piece," says Shahastra, "because I became a child again with the crayons."

168

FREE COLOR ME POLKA DOTS

after

169

> Dear Donna
> How To Do a T-Shirt.
> I had four permanent
> Markers. I had Red and
> Blue and I had green
> and yellow. And I colored
> it. I colored three flowers
> and four Butterflies.
> and I colored the laces.
> It was a white T-Shirt.
> And now its a colorful
> T-shirt.
>
> Love, Aimee

AIMEE'S PALETTE

Color Plate 11

Aimee, now eight years old, began designing with waterproof felt-tip markers a couple of years ago. She'll take anyone's old clothes and turn them into a rainbow with her drawings, always leaving her signature at the bottom. Mama Fran's T-shirt already had the outlines of the designs, which Aimee filled in with color, as one would do with a coloring book. Aimee wrote me a letter telling me how she did her own T-shirt.

She also drew her design right onto Grandpa's tie.

before

SAD BLOUSE TAKES ON SEX APPEAL

One day, foraging in a freestore, Barcat found this sexless pink blouse. It was too big and had absolutely no style. But there were redeeming features. The neckline was low and ruffled; the fabric, a harmless pink color. And it drip dried.

"I thought I'd just pare away the bulk," she says, "get rid of the floppiness, and maybe I'd have something. So I cut off the shapeless sleeves and widened the armhole by about 2", making the cut straight, not curved. I gave the armhole a $\frac{1}{4}$" hem.

Then $4\frac{1}{2}''$ from the bust dart, or about $6\frac{1}{2}''$ from the hemmed armhole, I cut away the bottom edge of the blouse. The edge was turned up to make a $\frac{3}{4}''$ casing. Right at the front, I left an opening through which to run a narrow cord to gather and tie the midriff top under the bustline. Last, I drew a flower design all around the collar with waterproof fabric markers (blue, yellow, red, purple, and green). Then I put a stripe around the armholes and down the front of the blouse where the buttonholes line up.''

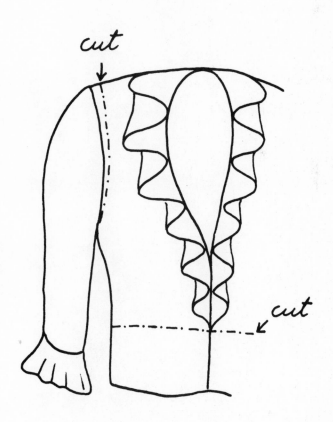

**SAD BLOUSE
TAKES ON
SEX APPEAL**

after

FREE

174

OLD LEATHER AND NEW PAINT

Harriet paints beautiful mythical animals butterflies, birds, and flowers on any surface that pleases her. Old leather is a favorite canvas for her. She has made an old fur coat (turned inside out), a well-worn pair of boots, a used handbag, and a child's suede skirt (found at the Salvation Army for four dollars) into works of art.

She used acrylic paints. The leather was not given any special treatment, but merely wiped clean with a soft dry cloth. As Harriet is an experienced artist, she painted directly on the surface, letting the leather inspire her. But she suggests that beginners draw their designs on paper, then cut them out and draw around them. It's best to keep your pattern simple, if you doubt your artistic ability. Curvy patterns are better than geometrics, in Harriet's opinion.

You can also trace a design from a book or magazine, using the grid method for enlarging or reducing designs (see page 200). It might be considered a drawback that painted-on leather can't be dry-cleaned. But Harriet doesn't consider it a problem. "You just wear and wear it and let it improve with the patina of age. Occasionally, you can take a paintbrush and touch it up a bit."

176   Color Plate 7   **after**

after

before

$4

178

after

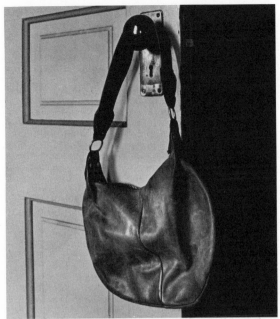

before

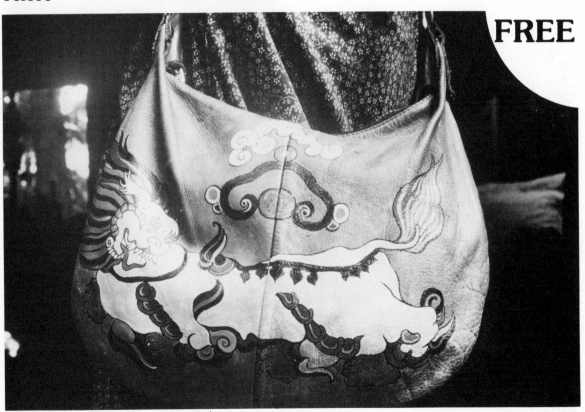

FREE

after

179

before

75¢

CHEINA'S FRANGIPANI SHOES

Cheina, an artist who lives in Key West, where the fragrant smell of frangipani lingers, has acrylic-painted that sweet white flower onto suede wedgies found in near-new shape at a thrift shop for seventy-five cents.

180

after

Stitch Ons

Colorful threads stitched this way and that bring new life to old garments. Look for strong fabrics—old favorites like muslin, chambray, denim, or corduroy—to take the needle and thread. Fragile antiques may tear when embroidered.

Your local library has a wealth of instructive embroidery books, I'll bet. Begin with easy stitches and work up to the more elaborate ones. It's a lovely and time-honored pastime.

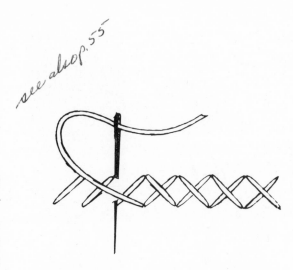

see also p. 55

CROSS STITCH

For cross stitch rows, make a row of diagonal stitches. Cross each stitch with another diagonal stitch.

PARVATI'S GREEN HILLS

Parvati paid one dollar for this mussed-up muslin. The fabric was tough, like new, so she used it for a needlework canvas. With tiny crossstitches and cotton floss she sketched in green rolling hills on the yoke.

"I use embroidery to bring old clothes back to life," said Parvati, who wears the smock. "This old muslin was like a canvas for me. My eye told me what design the garment would take and what it wouldn't. The rolling-hills design was built on the character of the garment."

before

181

Right

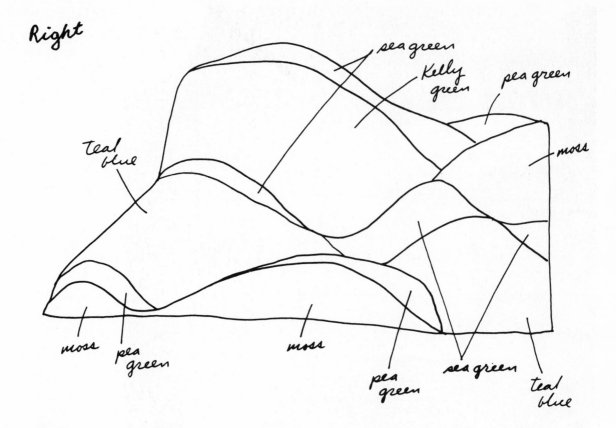

sea green

Kelly green

pea green

Teal blue

moss

moss

pea green

moss

pea green

sea green

Teal blue

Left

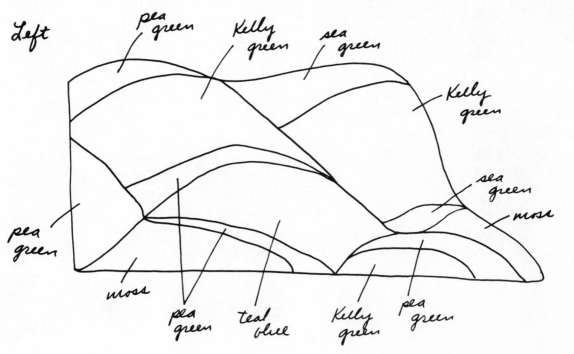

pea green

Kelly green

sea green

Kelly green

pea green

sea green

moss

moss

pea green

teal blue

Kelly green

pea green

183

BUTTERFLY LANDS ON OLD WORKSHIRT

The blue softens with age. The fabric comfortably wrinkles and clings to your skin. The shirt accentuates the body and character of the person who wears it. On men or women, there is a sexiness to these old shirts that words fail to describe. Parvati found this one at a freestore, and added her touch: embroidery—a butterfly, a daisy, and a little green.

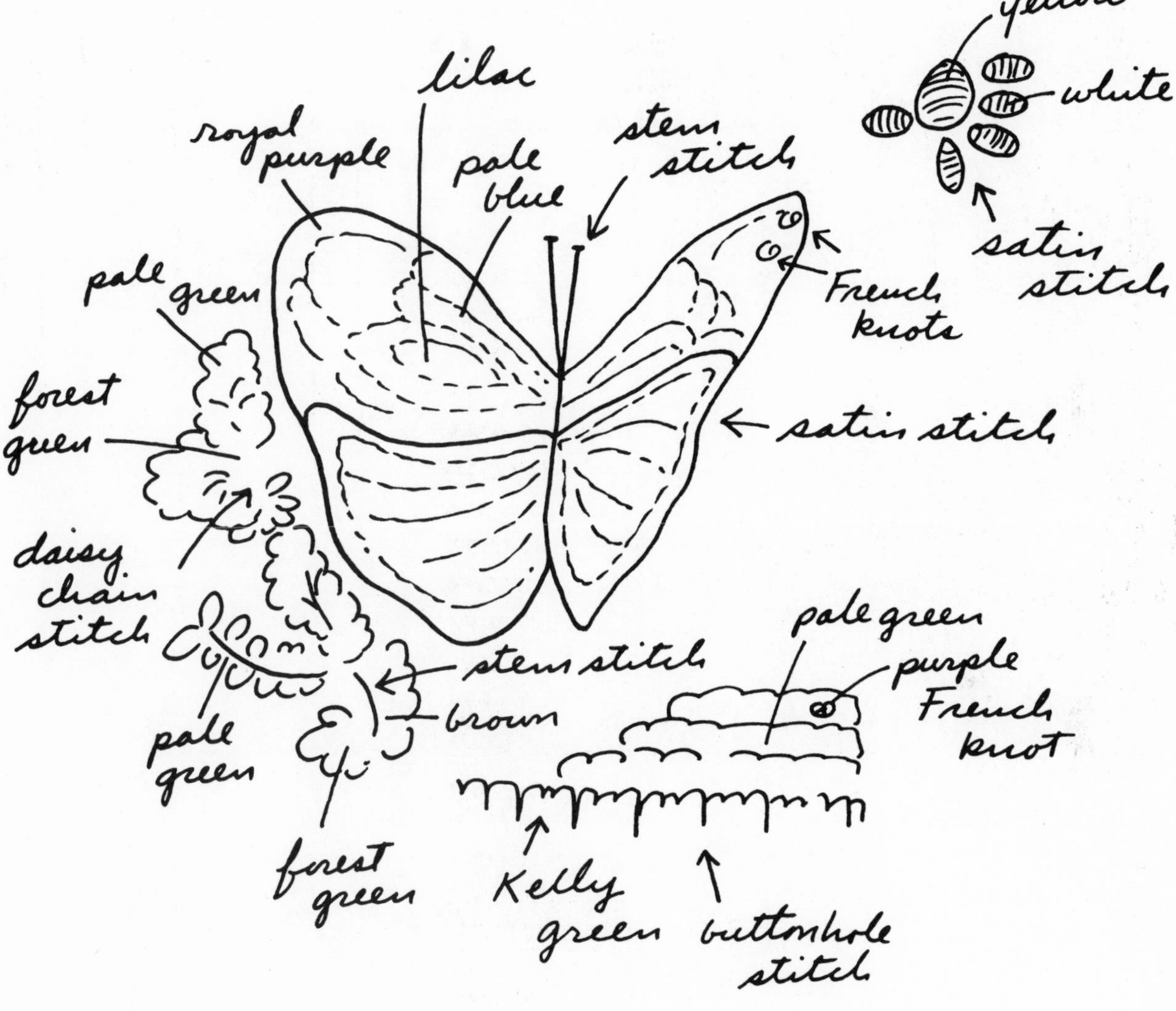

yellow

white

satin
stitch

lilac

stem
stitch

royal
purple

pale
blue

French
knots

pale green

satin stitch

forest
green

daisy
chain
stitch

pale
green

stem stitch

brown

pale green

purple

French
knot

forest
green

Kelly
green

buttonhole
stitch

185

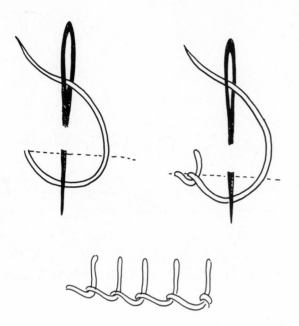

BUTTONHOLE STITCH

Bring thread up. Make a verticle stitch a short distance away with the needle point coming out on level with the up-coming thread. Be sure needle passes over loop of thread and pull through. Continue in the same manner.

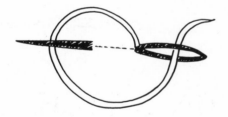

CHAIN STITCH

For first stitch, bring thread up. Insert needle next to the thread and bring it out a short distance away. Be sure that thread loops under the needle point. Pull needle through. Continue so that stitches interlock.

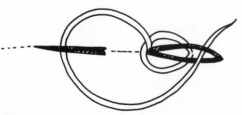

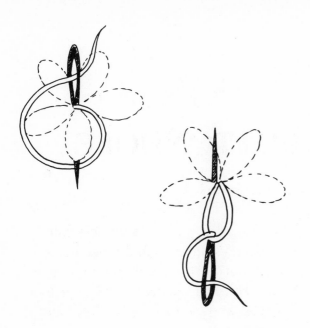

LAZY DAISY

A variation of the chain stitch, begin as in the chain. Instead of continuing with interlocking stitches, tie off each chain stitch by taking a tiny stitch at the top of the loop. Fan stitches around a center point.

STEM STITCH

Insert needle and bring it back out in the middle of the stitch. Pull thread through. Continue in the same manner. Be consistent about holding the thread above or below the stitch being made.

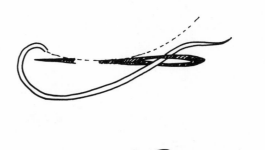

SATIN STITCH

Bring thread up. Insert needle a distance away and carry thread behind the work to bring thread up in position for the next stitch. Stitches should be close together to make a smooth surface.

Note: For instructions on making the French knots, see page 55.

187

BUTTERFLY
LANDS ON
OLD
WORKSHIRT

after

FREE

188

5

CLOTHES WITH A PAST

In Grandma's attic, Mother's bottom drawer, or hanging forlorn on a thrift shop hanger may be a genuine historic find. A look through a book on costume history will tell you what you have. Look for research material at your local library. Or investigate the nearest museum. Many of them are building up their costume collections and have a wealth of information gathered from fashion magazines dating back to the nineteenth century.

Some of these clothes are quite valuable investments—Bobbie's $1000 Fortuny (page 193) for one. As with any rare antique, the value increases with age. I have a friend who supports herself by buying old clothes (she knows her stuff) and reselling them at more than twice the price.

Beside the monetary realities, there's the pure drama of wearing them. There is no show stopper like walking into a room in a shimmering bit of 1910 fluff.

Speeded-Up Loungewear

Lounging jackets and pajama coats are from an era when there was all the time in the world. They were for languishing in bed over breakfast trays or sitting up late reading or hanging around eating chocolates, pin curling your hair, and drying your nails.

Those were the days before the beat got faster and, somehow, days got shorter. Now you don't lounge in loungewear. You put it on and race about in it.

$7

LATE 1930'S LOUNGING JACKET

Bobbie Abrams shows her late 1930's lounging jacket worn over black silk pants.

190

75¢

MID 1940'S LOUNGING PAJAMAS

Bobbie Pearlman wears her 1940's navy rayon pajamas over a white leotard. They cost seventy-five cents at the Salvation Army.

$5

EARLY 1950'S LOUNGE COAT

Corinne steps out in a 1950's apricot-colored rayon satin lounge coat.

BOBBIE'S FIFTY DOLLAR KIMONO

$50

Kimonos are hot stuff. Not since the Russo-Japanese War of 1904–1905 have kimonos flourished as they do today. You occasionally find a genuine old one for a decent price, but they're going fast. Even imitations from recent years are quickly grabbed. So anything with an oriental motif is a rare find. This one, a real antique, cost fifty dollars.

"Unless you're an expert on dyes, it's hard to date kimonos," says Bobbie. "But I know mine is a deep purple Icat weave, and that makes it valuable. Even though I paid more for it than anything else in my wardrobe, it's a bargain. I wear it as an evening coat. With fifty evenings behind it, it's cost me a dollar a time."

192

A GENUINE FORTUNY (1930-1939)

Bobbie's boyfriend is named Nicky. His mother was a prima ballerina with the Stuttgart Ballet. Each year, she bought her clothes in Italy. And sometime between 1930 and 1939 she bought this teal blue Fortuny, which Bobbie now owns. The gown was recently estimated to be worth $1000.

"Mario Fortuny had a special way of pleating silk," says Bobbie. "When he died, the method died with him. New York's Metropolitan Museum has been trying to figure out the proper formula for years. It's apparently some weird secret they can't find."

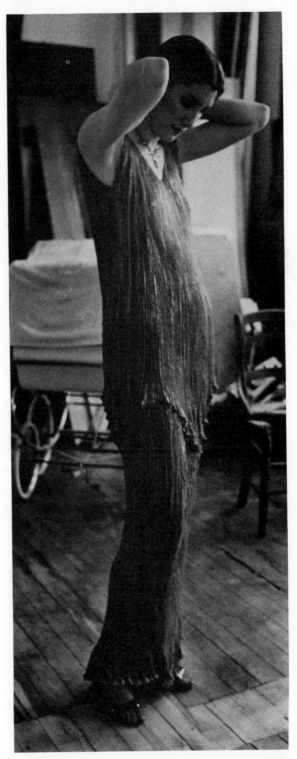

193

MY MOTHER'S DRESS

"In the Forties my mother danced at Roseland in this dress," says Corinne. "I feel vivacious in it—real nightlife, it says. Clothes used to be attuned to the female emotions. They felt sensuous and seductive. Today I can get that feeling if I wear old clothes. When I wear this dress, I feel feminine sexy. When I wear a suit like Lauren Bacall wore in the movies, I feel—well—tough sexy."

GREAT-AUNT LILY'S INAUGURAL BALL GOWN (1893)

Harriet models the handmade, cream-colored lace dress that her Great-aunt Lily wore to Grover Cleveland's Inaugural Ball in 1893. She was the wife of young Senator Hart from Hackensack, New Jersey, and had a wasp waist. Harriet does, too. So she wore the inherited ball gown as her own wedding dress in 1972.

A 1910 GARDEN PARTY GOWN

Alex inherited the dress from her mother, who got it from *her* godmother long before Alex's mother met Alex's father, and Alex was born. The dress is a soft, sheer, white cotton. "The general fragile look," says Alex. There were a few tears in the skirt, but these were mended by appliquéing lace doilies over them. "When I don't show up in jeans at a party, I wear this dress. There's nothing in between for me," says Alex, who wears the dress on the stoop of her house.

195

BABY ANTIQUES

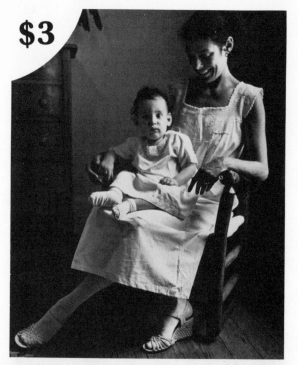

$3

Bobbie's baby Lexie has a romantic collection of antique clothes which teams up nicely with Bobbie's own clothing collection. Here, Mama wears a one-hundred-year-old chemise (two dollars) to match Lexie's baby nightie (one dollar). Both were bought at a Saturday flea market, as were the Edwardian romper suits and coat. "Everything my child owns is from the Salvation Army," says Bobbie. "I pick up terrific playclothes for twenty-five to fifty cents. And Lexie has quite a collection of secondhand knits. They'd cost a fortune anywhere else."

$2 **$5** **$2**

OLD HANDWORK APRON

Sometimes an old apron is so exquisite that there is nothing to do but tie it on over some special at-home outfit. This delicately hand-embroidered one was bought for eight dollars. Harriet washed it carefully in cold-water soap, ironed it, and tied it over a black velvet skirt.

$8

FIBER CARE CHART

Fiber	General Care	Special Instructions	Fiber	General Care	Special Instructions
acrylic	Most items should be washed in warm water by hand. Squeeze out water, don't wring. Smooth item and dry on hanger. If labeled for machine washing, use warm water, machine dry at low, and remove from dryer as soon as tumbling cycle is over.	Dry knitted items flat (they'll stretch otherwise). Static electricity build-up can be reduced by using fabric softener in every four or five washings, whether by hand or machine.		Some white polyesters pick up color from other fabrics; wash separately if this would be objectionable. Polyester fabrics can be dry cleaned but watch prints—some color substances often used on printed polyesters are injured by dry cleaning.	
cotton	Most 100% cottons can be washed by machine at the regular cycle with hot water, and dried at the regular setting. Use chlorine bleach only on whites and colored fabrics which you have tested for color retention. High temperature iron setting may be used. Wash cotton knits by hand.	Don't assume that all cotton fabrics are colorfast. Check the label or test a small portion; if the color runs, have the item dry cleaned.	rayon	Dry cleaning is definitely safest for rayon; however, if washing, wash by hand in lukewarm water. Do not wring or twist, and don't use chlorine bleach. Smooth the item, hang on hanger to dry, press while still damp on the wrong side with a moderate iron or use a pressing cloth on the right side.	Notice caution on the use of chlorine bleach.
linen	Machine wash in hot water, dry at regular cycle. Dark colors should be washed in water of a lower temperature to keep them from fading. Dry cleaning is especially satisfactory for color and shape retention.	Do not bleach colored linens.	silk	Dry cleaning is best for silk, although some silks can be hand washed (only if so labeled). Squeeze suds through fabric, do not wring or twist. Iron on the wrong side. To avoid water spotting, do not steam when pressing. Iron at medium temperature.	Never use chlorine bleach on silk.
nylon	Most items can be machine washed in warm water and tumble dried at low setting. Remove from dryer promptly to avoid heat-set wrinkles. If ironing is desired, use only a warm iron. Nylon tends to pick up colors from other fabrics if not washed separately. Sponge upholstery and rugs or use special cleaners for these items.	Static electricity can be reduced by the use of fabric softener in every four or five washings.	wool	Woven woolens should be dry cleaned, except for those labeled "washable." Follow care instructions on such woolens exactly. Machine-made knitted woolens should also be dry cleaned, unless labeled "washable," in which case follow label instructions. The dry cleaner should be told these fabrics are woolens to ensure the proper technique is used in cleaning and drying. Hand wash socks, mittens, and hand-knitted items in lukewarm or cold water using special soap for wool.	Never use chlorine bleach on wool. Dry knits flat to avoid stretching.
polyester	Machine washing at a warm setting with drying at a low temperature is recommended for polyester. Remove items from the dryer promptly to avoid heat-set wrinkles. Iron with a moderately warm iron.	Avoid over-drying of polyester and especially of polyester knits—it will give the effect of shrinkage. Notice caution on dry cleaning of polyesters.			

198

STAIN REMOVAL CHART

Stain	Removal method
ballpoint pen ink	Ballpoint pen ink comes out quite easily when sponged with rubbing alcohol. On a washable fabric, any stain which remains should be rubbed with soap or a detergent and then the fabric should be washed. The same method should be used on non-washable items, followed by sponging with a mild detergent solution of 1 teaspoon detergent to 1 cup of water.
blood	Washable fabrics should be soaked in cold water immediately. If they do not respond to cold water, an enzyme pre-soak (when available) should be used. The fabrics should then be washed in the usual way. Non-washable items should be sponged with cold water followed by a mild detergent solution (1 teaspoon detergent to 1 cup of water). If the detergent solution doesn't work, try a solution of 1 tablespoon ammonia in a cup of water—and if that changes the color of the item, follow it up by sponging with $\frac{1}{4}$ cup white vinegar in 1 cup of water to bring back the original color. Test both the ammonia solution and the vinegar solution in some inconspicuous spot before using on the stain.
candle wax	Follow instructions for chewing gum, below.
chewing gum	Chewing gum can be removed from most fabrics if it is first hardened by rubbing it with an ice cube and then scraped off with a blunt knife or your fingernail. This takes time and patience but it does work. In desperate cases, you can try sponging the gum with a nonflammable cleaning fluid, but this can spread the stain.
coffee, tea	Simple washing will usually remove coffee and tea stains on washable fabrics. On non-washable fabrics, sponge with cold water first, then try mild detergent solution of 1 teaspoon detergent to 1 cup of water.
cream, milk	Washing will remove cream and milk from washable fabrics. On non-washable fabrics, start by wiping with a damp sponge. If that fails, shake cornstarch or white talcum powder onto the stain, allow to dry thoroughly, then use a brush or vacuum to remove the residue.

Stain	Removal method
greasy stains, including lipstick, tar	Start by following the ice-cube method given for chewing gum, then use lighter fluid to remove remaining stain on both washable and non-washable fabrics.
nail polish	Nail polish remover will remove nail polish from most fabrics, but NEVER use it on acetate or triacetate. On these fabrics, try to scrape the polish off with a blunt knife or fingernail.
paint (oil based)	See instructions for nail polish, above.
paint (water based)	If the paint is still wet, sponge with water trying not to spread the stain further. If the paint is dry, nothing (including dry cleaning) will get it out, but you may be able to scrape some off the surface with a blunt knife or your fingernail.
perspiration	Certain man-made fibers seem to hold perspiration odors longer than other fabrics; although a stain will come out with washing, the odor may not. Rub the area of the odor with a deodorant soap before washing.
urine, vomit, mucous	On washable fabrics, soak in an enzyme pre-soak (if possible) then wash using a suitable bleach (chlorine or oxygen type). On non-washable items, such as rugs, sponge first with mild detergent solution (1 teaspoon detergent to a cup of water) and rinse. If that doesn't work, try white vinegar solution—$\frac{1}{4}$ cup white vinegar to 1 cup water. If this solution changes the color, try to neutralize it with an ammonia solution of 1 tablespoon ammonia to 1 cup water. Test both the ammonia solution and the vinegar solution in an inconspicuous spot before using on the stain.

Reprinted from:
The Butterick Fabric Handbook
A Consumer's Guide to Fabrics
for Clothing and Home Furnishings
Edited by Irene Kleeberg © 1976
Butterick Publishing
161 Sixth Avenue
New York, New York 10013

ENLARGING OR REDUCING DESIGNS

Determine how much to enlarge or reduce the design by considering the size of the completed project and the size relationship between the completed size and the design size.

Place a grid over the design. The grid should consist of carefully measured exact squares.

Prepare a grid with the same number of squares as the grid superimposed over the design.
Number the squares along one side and the top of both grids for easy reference while drawing.

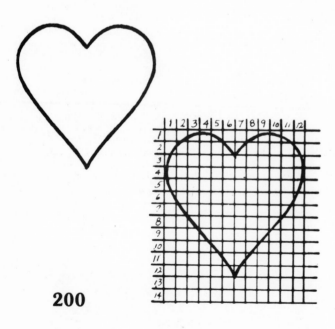

To enlarge design:
The prepared grid should have larger squares than the original design. If the design to be enlarged is superimposed with a grid of $\frac{1}{8}''$ squares, translate it onto a grid of $\frac{1}{4}''$, $\frac{1}{2}''$, or $1''$ squares.

To reduce design:
The prepared grid should have smaller squares than the original design. If the design to be reduced is superimposed with a grid of $1''$ squares, translate it onto a grid of $\frac{1}{2}''$, $\frac{1}{4}''$, or $\frac{1}{8}''$ squares.

Note: A short cut is to overlay the original design with graph paper or fine wire screen. The design may be drawn onto the graph paper, so that the need to painstakingly construct grids is eliminated.

Translate the original outline to the grid one square at a time.